SENTENCE TRANSFORMATION

THINGS YOU SHOULD KNOW
(QUESTIONS AND ANSWERS)

By Rumi Michael Leigh

Introduction

I would like to thank you for purchasing this book, *"Sentence transformation, things you should know (questions and answers)"*.

This book will help you understand, revise, and have a good general knowledge and understanding of the basics of sentence transformation.

I hope you enjoy it!

Table of Contents

Chapter 1: Rewrite the sentence(s) using a different verb tense

Exercise 1: Rewrite the sentences using a different verb tense:

Questions

a) She is currently studying for her exams.
b) The team will be playing in the championship game tomorrow.

Answers

a) She has been studying for her exams for a while now.
b) The team has been preparing for the championship game tomorrow.

Chapter 2: Rewrite the sentence(s) using a different grammatical structure

Exercise 1: Rewrite the sentence using a different grammatical structure:

Question

a) John loves pizza more than anything else in the world.

Answer

a) More than anything else in the world, John loves pizza.

Chapter 3: Rewrite the sentence(s) using a different word order

Exercise 1: Rewrite the sentence using a different word order:

Question

a) The cat chased the mouse around the house.

Answer

a) Around the house, the mouse was chased by the cat.

Chapter 4: Rewrite the sentence(s) using a different voice

Exercise 1: Rewrite the sentences using a different voice

Questions

a) The teacher gave the students a test.
b) The company hired a new CEO.
c) The waiter served us our food.
d) The company awarded him with a promotion.
e) The chef cooked the meal to perfection.

Answers

a) The students were given a test by the teacher.
b) A new CEO was hired by the company.
c) We were served our food by the waiter.
d) He was awarded a promotion by the company.
e) The meal was cooked to perfection by the chef.

Exercise 2: Rewrite the sentences using a different voice

Questions

a) The teacher graded the exams.
b) The doctor prescribed the medication.
c) The company offered him a job.
d) The company will hire a new employee.
e) The teacher asked the students a question.

Answers

a) The exams were graded by the teacher.
b) The medication was prescribed by the doctor.

c) He was offered a job by the company.

d) A new employee will be hired by the company.

e) A question was asked to the students by the teacher.

Exercise 3: Rewrite the sentences using a different voice

Questions

a) The waiter brought us our food.

b) The company will send the documents via email.

c) The chef prepared the meal.

d) The company offered her a promotion.

e) The student asked the teacher a question.

Answers

a) We were brought our food by the waiter.

b) The documents will be sent via email by the company.

c) The meal was prepared by the chef.

d) She was offered a promotion by the company.

e) A question was asked to the teacher by the student.

Exercise 4: Rewrite the sentences using a different voice

Questions

a) The artist painted the portrait.

b) The waiter served the food.

c) The company made a decision.

d) The teacher explained the lesson.

e) The musician played the guitar.

Answers

a) The portrait was painted by the artist.

b) The food was served by the waiter.

c) A decision was made by the company.

d) The lesson was explained by the teacher.

e) The guitar was played by the musician.

Exercise 5: Rewrite the sentences using a different voice

Questions

a) The company hired a new employee.

b) The coach trained the team.

c) The dog chased the cat.

d) The writer penned the novel.

e) The chef cooked the meal.

Answers

a) A new employee was hired by the company.

b) The team was trained by the coach.

c) The cat was chased by the dog.

d) The novel was penned by the writer.

e) The meal was cooked by the chef.

Exercise 6: Rewrite the sentences using a different voice

Questions

a) The company developed the product.

b) The artist painted the portrait.

c) The children broke the vase.

d) The teacher graded the papers.

e) The mechanic fixed the car.

Answers

a) The product was developed by the company.
b) The portrait was painted by the artist.
c) The vase was broken by the children.
d) The papers were graded by the teacher.
e) The car was fixed by the mechanic.

Exercise 7: Rewrite the sentences using a different voice

Questions

a) The students wrote the essay.
b) The company hired the new employee.
c) The singer performed the song.
d) Original: The artist drew the portrait.
e) Original: The teacher explained the lesson.

Answers

a) The essay was written by the students.
b) The new employee was hired by the company.
c) The song was performed by the singer.
d) The portrait was drawn by the artist.
e) The lesson was explained by the teacher.

Exercise 8: Rewrite the sentences using a different voice

Questions

a) The chef cooked the meal.
b) The student wrote the essay.
c) The doctor treated the patient.
d) The teacher assigned the homework.

e) The artist painted the picture.

Answers

a) The meal was cooked by the chef.
b) The essay was written by the student.
c) The patient was treated by the doctor.
d) The homework was assigned by the teacher.
e) The picture was painted by the artist.

Exercise 9: Rewrite the sentences using a different voice

Questions

a) The waiter served the food.
b) The doctor prescribed the medicine.
c) The teacher explained the lesson.
d) The artist sketched the portrait.
e) The chef cooked the meal.

Answers

a) The food was served by the waiter.
b) The medicine was prescribed by the doctor.
c) The lesson was explained by the teacher.
d) The portrait was sketched by the artist.
e) The meal was cooked by the chef.

Exercise 10: Rewrite the sentences using a different voice

Questions

a) The doctor examined the patient.
b) The teacher graded the papers.

c) The artist painted the portrait.

d) The company developed the software.

e) The team won the championship.

Answers

a) The patient was examined by the doctor.

b) The papers were graded by the teacher.

c) The portrait was painted by the artist.

d) The software was developed by the company.

e) The championship was won by the team.

Exercise 11: Rewrite the sentences using a different voice

Questions

a) The company designed the product.

b) The chef prepared the meal.

c) The teacher gave the students a quiz.

d) The team played the game.

e) The company sold the product.

Answers

a) The product was designed by the company.

b) The meal was prepared by the chef.

c) The students were given a quiz by the teacher.

d) The game was played by the team.

e) The product was sold by the company.

Exercise 12: Rewrite the sentences using a different voice

Questions

a) The singer performed the song.

b) The student asked the teacher a question.

c) The artist painted the picture.

d) The chef cooked the meal.

e) The students are reading the book.

Answers

a) The song was performed by the singer.

b) The teacher was asked a question by the student.

c) The picture was painted by the artist.

d) The meal was cooked by the chef.

e) The book is being read by the students.

Exercise 13: Rewrite the sentences using a different voice

Questions

a) The company hired the new employee.

b) The teacher is grading the papers.

c) The company will be announcing the winner tomorrow.

d) The chef will prepare the meal.

e) The doctor will examine the patient.

Answers

a) The new employee was hired by the company.

b) The papers are being graded by the teacher.

c) The winner will be announced by the company tomorrow.

d) The meal will be prepared by the chef.

e) The patient will be examined by the doctor.

Exercise 14: Rewrite the sentences using a different voice

Questions

a) The company is designing the new product.

b) The company is producing the new movie.

c) The teacher is explaining the lesson.

d) The company is building the new office.

e) The artist is painting a portrait.

Answers

a) The new product is being designed by the company.

b) The new movie is being produced by the company.

c) The lesson is being explained by the teacher.

d) The new office is being built by the company.

e) A portrait is being painted by the artist.

Exercise 15: Rewrite the sentences using a different voice

Questions

a) The waiter is serving the customers.

b) The company is launching a new product.

c) The singer is performing the new song.

d) The chef is cooking the meal.

e) The teacher is grading the papers.

Answers

a) The customers are being served by the waiter.

b) A new product is being launched by the company.

c) The new song is being performed by the singer.

d) The meal is being cooked by the chef.

e) The papers are being graded by the teacher.

Exercise 16: Rewrite the sentences using a different voice

Questions

a) The company is designing a new product.
b) The doctor is examining the patient.
c) The artist is painting a portrait.
d) The company is producing a new line of products.
e) The chef is cooking the meal.

Answers

a) A new product is being designed by the company.
b) The patient is being examined by the doctor.
c) A portrait is being painted by the artist.
d) A new line of products is being produced by the company.
e) The meal is being cooked by the chef.

Exercise 17: Rewrite the sentences using a different voice

Questions

a) The teacher is grading the exams.
b) The author wrote the book.
c) The mechanic is repairing the car.
d) The artist painted the picture.
e) The chef is making the soup.

Answers

a) The exams are being graded by the teacher.
b) The book was written by the author.
c) The car is being repaired by the mechanic.
d) The picture was painted by the artist.

e) The soup is being made by the chef.

Exercise 18: Rewrite the sentences using a different voice

Questions

a) The doctor will examine the patient.
b) The teacher is grading the tests.
c) The company is hiring new employees.
d) The artist will paint the portrait.
e) The company designed the new product.

Answers

a) The patient will be examined by the doctor.
b) The tests are being graded by the teacher.
c) New employees are being hired by the company.
d) The portrait will be painted by the artist.
e) The new product was designed by the company.

Exercise 19: Rewrite the sentences using a different voice

Questions

a) The teacher is explaining the lesson.
b) The band will perform at the concert.
c) The committee has approved the proposal.
d) The company will release a new product next month.
e) The company hired a new employee.

Answers

a) The lesson is being explained by the teacher.
b) The concert will feature a performance by the band.

c) The proposal has been approved by the committee.

d) A new product will be released by the company next month.

e) A new employee was hired by the company.

Exercise 20: Rewrite the sentences using a different voice

Questions

a) The company designed a new logo.

b) The company produces high-quality products.

c) The company sells organic produce.

d) The company provides excellent customer service.

Answers

a) A new logo was designed by the company.

b) High-quality products are produced by the company.

c) Organic produce is sold by the company.

d) Excellent customer service is provided by the company.

Chapter 5: Rewrite the sentence(s) using a different degree of comparison

Exercise 1: Rewrite the sentences using a different degree of comparison

Questions

a) Original: This is the best ice cream I've ever had.
b) Original: The test was harder than I expected.
c) Original: She is the most talented musician in the school.
d) Original: This book is the best one I've ever read.
e) Original: This restaurant is the busiest one in town.

Answers

a) Rewritten: This ice cream is better than any I've ever had.
b) Rewritten: The test was more difficult than I expected.
c) Rewritten: She is more talented than any other musician in the school.
d) Rewritten: This book is better than any other book I've ever read.
e) Rewritten: This restaurant is busier than any other in town.

Exercise 2: Rewrite the sentences using a different degree of comparison

Questions

a) Original: This phone is the most expensive one on the market.
b) Original: She is the tallest person in her family.
c) Original: This car is the fastest one in its class.
d) Original: She is the smartest person in her class.
e) Original: This house is the most expensive one on the block.

Answers

a) Rewritten: This phone is more expensive than any other on the market.

b) Rewritten: She is taller than anyone else in her family.

c) Rewritten: This car is faster than any other in its class.

d) Rewritten: She is smarter than anyone else in her class.

e) Rewritten: This house is more expensive than any other on the block.

Exercise 3: Rewrite the sentences using a different degree of comparison

Questions

a) Original: This laptop is the lightest one in its class.

b) Original: This phone is the thinnest one on the market.

c) Original: This laptop is the most expensive one in the store.

d) Original: He is the best athlete on the team.

e) Original: This book is the longest one in the series.

Answers

a) Rewritten: This laptop is lighter than any other in its class.

b) Rewritten: This phone is thinner than any other on the market.

c) Rewritten: This laptop is more expensive than any other in the store.

d) Rewritten: He is a better athlete than anyone else on the team.

e) Rewritten: This book is longer than any other in the series.

Exercise 4: Rewrite the sentences using a different degree of comparison

Questions

a) Original: This car is the slowest one on the highway.

b) Original: This watch is the most expensive one in the store.

c) Original: This shirt is the softest one in the store.

d) Original: This car is the most reliable one on the market.

e) Original: This book is the most popular one in the series.

Answers

a) Rewritten: This car is slower than any other on the highway.

b) Rewritten: This watch is more expensive than any other in the store.

c) Rewritten: This shirt is softer than any other in the store.

d) Rewritten: This car is more reliable than any other on the market.

e) Rewritten: This book is more popular than any other in the series.

Exercise 5: Rewrite the sentences using a different degree of comparison

Questions

a) Original: This car is the fastest one on the road.

b) Original: This house is the largest one on the block.

c) Original: This restaurant is the most popular one in town.

d) Original: This laptop is the most expensive one in the store.

e) Original: This phone is the thinnest one on the market.

Answers

a) Rewritten: This car is faster than any other on the road.

b) Rewritten: This house is larger than any other on the block.

c) Rewritten: This restaurant is more popular than any other in town.

d) Rewritten: This laptop is more expensive than any other in the store.

e) Rewritten: This phone is thinner than any other on the market.

Exercise 6: Rewrite the sentences using a different degree of comparison

Questions

a) Original: This computer is the fastest one in the store.

b) Original: This book is the longest one in the series.

c) Original: This car is the most reliable one in the lot.

d) Original: This city is the busiest one in the state.

e) Original: This book is the most interesting one I have ever read.

Answers

a) Rewritten: This computer is faster than any other in the store.

b) Rewritten: This book is longer than any other in the series.

c) Rewritten: This car is more reliable than any other in the lot.

d) Rewritten: This city is busier than any other in the state.

e) Rewritten: This book is more interesting than any other I have ever read.

Exercise 7: Rewrite the sentences using a different degree of comparison

Questions

a) Original: This movie is the funniest one I have ever seen.

b) Original: This car is the most expensive one in the showroom.

c) Original: This cake is the sweetest one I have ever tasted.

d) Original: This building is the tallest one in the city.

e) Original: This dress is the most expensive one in the store.

Answers

a) Rewritten: This movie is funnier than any other I have ever seen.

b) Rewritten: This car is more expensive than any other in the showroom.

c) Rewritten: This cake is sweeter than any other I have ever tasted.

d) Rewritten: This building is taller than any other in the city.

e) Rewritten: This dress is more expensive than any other in the store.

Exercise 8: Rewrite the sentences using a different degree of comparison

Questions

a) Original: This restaurant has the best food in town.

b) Original: This car is the fastest one in the race.

c) Original: This painting is the most beautiful one in the gallery.

d) Original: This flower is the prettiest one in the garden.

e) Original: This tree is the tallest one in the park.

Answers

a) Rewritten: This restaurant has better food than any other in town.
b) Rewritten: This car is faster than any other in the race.
c) Rewritten: This painting is more beautiful than any other in the gallery.
d) Rewritten: This flower is prettier than any other in the garden.
e) Rewritten: This tree is taller than any other in the park.

Exercise 9: Rewrite the sentences using a different degree of comparison

Questions

a) Original: This car is the most expensive one in the showroom.
b) Original: This building is the tallest one in the city.
c) Original: This river is the widest one in the country.
d) Original: This restaurant is the busiest one in town.
e) Original: This computer is the fastest one in the store.

Answers

a) Rewritten: This car is more expensive than any other in the showroom.
b) Rewritten: This building is taller than any other in the city.
c) Rewritten: This river is wider than any other in the country.
d) Rewritten: This restaurant is busier than any other in town.
e) Rewritten: This computer is faster than any other in the store.

Exercise 10: Rewrite the sentences using a different degree of comparison

Questions

a) Original: This cake is the sweetest one I've ever tasted.
b) Original: This dog is the most obedient one in the training class.

c) Original: This dress is the prettiest one in the store.

d) Original: This city is the most populous one in the state.

e) Original: This car is the fastest one on the road.

Answers

a) Rewritten: This cake is sweeter than any other I've ever tasted.

b) Rewritten: This dog is more obedient than any other in the training class.

c) Rewritten: This dress is prettier than any other in the store.

d) Rewritten: This city is more populous than any other in the state.

e) Rewritten: This car is faster than any other on the road.

Exercise 11: Rewrite the sentences using a different degree of comparison

Questions

a) Original: This book is the longest one I've ever read.

b) Original: This building is the tallest one in the city.

c) Original: This meal is the most delicious one I've ever had.

d) Original: This cake is the sweetest one I've ever tasted.

e) Original: This city is the most expensive one in the country.

Answers

a) Rewritten: This book is longer than any other I've ever read.

b) Rewritten: This building is taller than any other in the city.

c) Rewritten: This meal is more delicious than any other I've ever had.

d) Rewritten: This cake is sweeter than any other I've ever tasted.

e) Rewritten: This city is more expensive than any other in the country.

Exercise 12: Rewrite the sentences using a different degree of comparison

Questions

a) Original: This car is the most expensive one on the lot.

b) Original: This sandwich is the biggest one I've ever seen.

c) Original: This shirt is the most comfortable one I own.

d) Original: This restaurant has the best pizza in town.

e) Original: This apartment is the most spacious one available.

Answers

a) Rewritten: This car is more expensive than any other on the lot.

b) Rewritten: This sandwich is larger than any other I've ever seen.

c) Rewritten: This shirt is more comfortable than any other I own.

d) Rewritten: This restaurant has better pizza than any other in town.

e) Rewritten: This apartment is more spacious than any other available.

Exercise 13: Rewrite the sentences using a different degree of comparison

Questions

a) Original: This jacket is the warmest one I own.

b) Original: This laptop is the fastest one available.

c) Original: This museum has the most interesting exhibits.

d) Original: This coffee is the strongest one they serve.

e) Original: This store has the best prices.

Answers

a) Rewritten: This jacket is warmer than any other I own.

b) Rewritten: This laptop is faster than any other available.

c) Rewritten: This museum has more interesting exhibits than any other.

d) Rewritten: This coffee is stronger than any other they serve.

e) Rewritten: This store has better prices than any other.

Exercise 14: Rewrite the sentences using a different degree of comparison

Questions

    a) Original: This phone is the most expensive one they sell.

    b) Original: This car is the most reliable one on the market.

    c) Original: This restaurant has the best service.

    d) Original: This jacket is the warmest one they have.

    e) Original: This book is the best one she has written.

Answers

    a) Rewritten: This phone is more expensive than any other they sell.

    b) Rewritten: This car is more reliable than any other on the market.

    c) Rewritten: This restaurant has better service than any other.

    d) Rewritten: This jacket is warmer than any other they have.

    e) Rewritten: This book is better than any other she has written.

Exercise 15: Rewrite the sentences using a different degree of comparison

Questions

    a) Original: This laptop is the fastest one they sell.

    b) Original: This movie is the most popular one in the theater.

    c) Original: This restaurant has the friendliest staff.

    d) Original: This car is the most expensive one in the lot.

    e) Original: This house is the biggest one on the block.

Answers

    a) Rewritten: This laptop is faster than any other they sell.

    b) Rewritten: This movie is more popular than any other in the theater.

    c) Rewritten: This restaurant has friendlier staff than any other.

    d) Rewritten: This car is more expensive than any other in the lot.

    e) Rewritten: This house is bigger than any other on the block.

Exercise 16: Rewrite the sentences using a different degree of comparison

Questions

a) Original: This phone is the smallest one they sell.
b) Original: This restaurant has the spiciest food.
c) Original: This car is the fastest one on the road.
d) Original: This book is the most interesting one I've ever read.
e) Original: This cake is the sweetest one I've ever tasted.

Answers

a) Rewritten: This phone is smaller than any other they sell.
b) Rewritten: This restaurant has spicier food than any other.
c) Rewritten: This car is faster than any other on the road.
d) Rewritten: This book is more interesting than any other I've ever read.
e) Rewritten: This cake is sweeter than any other I've ever tasted.

Exercise 17: Rewrite the sentences using a different degree of comparison

Questions

a) Original: This house is the biggest one on the block.
b) Original: This house is the most expensive one in the neighborhood.
c) Original: This car is the most reliable one on the market.
d) Original: This house is the most modern one in the neighborhood.
e) Original: This dress is the most elegant one in the store.

Answers

a) Rewritten: This house is bigger than any other on the block.
b) Rewritten: This house is more expensive than any other in the neighborhood.
c) Rewritten: This car is more reliable than any other on the market.
d) Rewritten: This house is more modern than any other in the neighborhood.

e) Rewritten: This dress is more elegant than any other in the store.

Exercise 18: Rewrite the sentences using a different degree of comparison

Questions

a) Original: This phone is the most expensive one in the store.
b) Original: This building is the tallest one in the city.
c) Original: This book is the most interesting one I have ever read.
d) Original: This car is the fastest one on the road.
e) Original: This book is the longest one in the series.
f) Original: This cake is the sweetest one I have ever tasted.
g) Original: This flower is the prettiest one in the garden.

Answers

a) Rewritten: This phone is more expensive than any other in the store.
b) Rewritten: This building is taller than any other in the city.
c) Rewritten: This book is more interesting than any other I have ever read.
d) Rewritten: This car is faster than any other on the road.
e) Rewritten: This book is longer than any other in the series.
f) Rewritten: This cake is sweeter than any other I have ever tasted.
g) Rewritten: This flower is prettier than any other in the garden.

Chapter 6: Rewrite the sentence(s) using a different conjunction

Exercise 1: Rewrite the sentences using a different conjunction

Questions

a) I can't go out tonight because I have to study.
b) I want to go to the movies and watch a romantic comedy.
c) I want to go to the gym, but I don't have time.
d) She wants to eat pizza for dinner, but she's trying to eat healthier.
e) I can't go to the party because I have to work.

Answers

a) Although I have to study, I wish I could go out tonight.
b) I want to go to the movies or watch a romantic comedy.
c) I want to go to the gym, although I don't have time.
d) She wants to eat pizza for dinner, while she's trying to eat healthier.
e) I can't go to the party, even though I want to.

Exercise 2: Rewrite the sentences using a different conjunction

Questions

a) She wants to go to the concert, but she can't afford it.
b) I want to go to the beach and swim in the ocean.
c) I need to study for my exam, so I can't go out tonight.
d) She wants to travel the world, but she can't afford it.
e) I want to go to the beach, but it's raining.

Answers

a) Although she wants to go to the concert, she can't afford it.
b) I want to go to the beach so that I can swim in the ocean.

c) Since I need to study for my exam, I can't go out tonight.

d) She wants to travel the world, although she can't afford it.

e) Despite wanting to go to the beach, it's raining.

Exercise 3: Rewrite the sentences using a different conjunction

Questions

a) She is studying for her exam, and she's nervous.

b) He wants to go to the concert, but he has to work.

c) She is tired, but she can't go to bed yet.

d) He wants to study abroad, so he is learning a new language.

e) She is going to the gym, and she will also go for a run.

Answers

a) She is studying for her exam, as she is nervous.

b) He wants to go to the concert, even though he has to work.

c) She is tired, although she can't go to bed yet.

d) He wants to study abroad, therefore he is learning a new language.

e) She is going to the gym, as well as going for a run.

Exercise 4: Rewrite the sentences using a different conjunction

Questions

a) She is happy, but she's still worried about the test.

b) He is going to the store, and he will also pick up some groceries.

c) He is working hard, but he is not making progress.

d) She wants to travel, but she doesn't have enough money.

e) She is tired, but she still wants to go to the party.

Answers

a) She is happy, despite being worried about the test.

b) He is going to the store, in addition to picking up some groceries.

c) He is working hard, yet he is not making progress.

d) She wants to travel, although she doesn't have enough money.

e) She is tired, yet she still wants to go to the party.

Exercise 5: Rewrite the sentences using a different conjunction

Questions

a) He was tired, so he went to bed early.

b) She is excited, and she can't wait to start her new job.

c) He is happy, but he wishes he could see his family more often.

d) She is studying hard, so she can get a good grade.

e) He was tired, yet he pushed himself to finish the project.

Answers

a) He was tired, therefore he went to bed early.

b) She is excited, and eager to start her new job.

c) He is happy, although he wishes he could see his family more often.

d) She is studying hard in order to get a good grade.

e) He was tired, but he pushed himself to finish the project.

Exercise 6: Rewrite the sentences using a different conjunction

Questions

a) He loves to travel, and he wants to visit every continent.

b) She loves to dance, but she is afraid of performing in front of an audience.

c) He is excited to start his new job, so he is preparing for it diligently.

d) She is busy, yet she always finds time for her hobbies.

e) She is a great athlete, and she trains every day.

Answers

a) He loves to travel, so he wants to visit every continent.
b) She loves to dance, although she is afraid of performing in front of an audience.
c) He is excited to start his new job and is preparing for it diligently.
d) She is busy, but she always finds time for her hobbies.
e) She is a great athlete, so she trains every day.

Exercise 7: Rewrite the sentences using a different conjunction

Questions

a) He is tired because he stayed up late.
b) She wants to go to the beach, but it is raining outside.
c) She is studying hard, for she wants to get good grades.
d) He is saving money, so he can buy a new car.
e) She wants to go to the party, but she has to finish her homework.

Answers

a) He is tired since he stayed up late.
b) She wants to go to the beach, although it is raining outside.
c) She is studying hard since she wants to get good grades.
d) He is saving money, in order to buy a new car.
e) She wants to go to the party, although she has to finish her homework.

Exercise 8: Rewrite the sentences using a different conjunction

Questions

a) He wants to travel the world, but he cannot afford it.
b) She is tired because she worked late.
c) She is studying for the exam, but she is feeling anxious.
d) He will go to the party if he finishes his work.

e) She needs to buy groceries, and she also needs to do laundry.

Answers

a) He wants to travel the world, though he cannot afford it.
b) She is tired since she worked late.
c) She is studying for the exam, yet she is feeling anxious.
d) He will go to the party provided he finishes his work.
e) She needs to buy groceries, as well as do laundry.

Exercise 9: Rewrite the sentences using a different conjunction

Questions

a) He loves to travel, but he hates packing.
b) She likes to read, and she also enjoys writing.
c) He will go to the concert if he can get a ticket.
d) She wants to go to the beach, but it's too far.
e) He is tired, so he is going to bed early.

Answers

a) He loves to travel, though he hates packing.
b) She likes to read, as well as enjoys writing.
c) He will go to the concert provided he can get a ticket.
d) She wants to go to the beach, although it's too far.
e) He is tired, hence he is going to bed early.

Exercise 10: Rewrite the sentences using a different conjunction

Questions

a) She is studying for the exam, yet she still feels unprepared.
b) I want to go on vacation, but I can't afford it.

c) The food is delicious, and it's also healthy.

d) She wants to travel, but she doesn't have the time.

e) He is tired, yet he is working overtime.

Answers

a) She is studying for the exam, still she feels unprepared.

b) I want to go on vacation, although I can't afford it.

c) The food is delicious, as well as healthy.

d) She wants to travel, though she doesn't have the time.

e) He is tired, still he is working overtime.

Exercise 11: Rewrite the sentences using a different conjunction

Questions

a) She is happy, but she is also nervous.

b) He is sick, so he is staying home from work.

c) She loves to dance, yet she never takes lessons.

d) He likes to swim, but he doesn't like to get his face wet.

e) She is tired, yet she is still working.

Answers

a) She is happy, and she is also nervous.

b) He is sick, therefore he is staying home from work.

c) She loves to dance, though she never takes lessons.

d) He likes to swim, although he doesn't like to get his face wet.

e) She is tired, but she is still working.

Exercise 12: Rewrite the sentences using a different conjunction

Questions

a) He wants to go to the party, and he wants to bring his friend.

b) She wants to buy the dress, but it's too expensive.

c) He is tired, so he is going to bed.

d) She is studying for the exam, yet she is still watching TV.

e) She wants to go to the beach, and she wants to go swimming.

Answers

a) He wants to go to the party, as well as bring his friend.

b) She wants to buy the dress, although it's too expensive.

c) He is tired, therefore he is going to bed.

d) She is studying for the exam, but she is still watching TV.

e) She wants to go to the beach, as well as go swimming.

Exercise 13: Rewrite the sentences using a different conjunction

Questions

a) He is hungry, so he is going to get something to eat.

b) She likes to go for walks, but she doesn't like to run.

c) She needs to finish her homework, or she will fail the class.

d) He wants to eat pizza, but he also wants to eat tacos.

e) She was tired, so she went to bed early.

Answers

a) He is hungry, therefore he is going to get something to eat.

b) She likes to go for walks, although she doesn't like to run.

c) She needs to finish her homework, otherwise she will fail the class.

d) He wants to eat pizza, as well as tacos.

e) She was tired, therefore she went to bed early.

Exercise 14: Rewrite the sentences using a different conjunction

Questions

a) He didn't study for the exam, yet he still passed.

b) She loves to read, and she also loves to write.

c) The food was good, but the service was slow.

d) She wants to go to the beach, and she also wants to go to the mountains.

e) The concert was loud, but it was also enjoyable.

Answers

a) He didn't study for the exam, nevertheless he still passed.

b) She loves to read, as well as write.

c) The food was good, although the service was slow.

d) She wants to go to the beach, as well as the mountains.

e) The concert was loud, yet it was enjoyable.

Exercise 15: Rewrite the sentences using a different conjunction

Questions

a) The dog barked loudly, so the neighbors complained.

b) She loves to dance, but she hates to sing.

c) He wants to learn to play the guitar, but he doesn't have time.

d) The weather was hot, so we went swimming.

e) She is a good student, and she always gets good grades.

Answers

a) The dog barked loudly, therefore the neighbors complained.

b) She loves to dance, although she hates to sing.

c) He wants to learn to play the guitar, yet he doesn't have time.

d) The weather was hot, therefore we went swimming.

e) She is a good student, as a result she always gets good grades.

Exercise 16: Rewrite the sentences using a different conjunction

Questions

   a) She was tired, so she went to bed early.
   b) He wanted to go for a walk, but it was raining.
   c) The dog was barking, so the man went to check on it.
   d) She worked hard, but she didn't get the promotion.
   e) He was tired, so he took a nap.

Answers

   a) She was tired, hence she went to bed early.
   b) He wanted to go for a walk, although it was raining.
   c) The dog was barking, therefore the man went to check on it.
   d) She worked hard, however she didn't get the promotion.
   e) He was tired, hence he took a nap.

Exercise 17: Rewrite the sentences using a different conjunction

Questions

   a) She's allergic to peanuts, so she can't eat peanut butter.
   b) She likes to read, but she doesn't have much free time.
   c) He was hungry, so he made a sandwich.
   d) She studied hard, but she failed the test.
   e) He loves pizza, and he eats it every week.

Answers

   a) She's allergic to peanuts; therefore, she can't eat peanut butter.
   b) She likes to read, although she doesn't have much free time.
   c) He was hungry, and he made a sandwich.
   d) She studied hard, yet she failed the test.

e) He loves pizza, so he eats it every week.

Exercise 18: Rewrite the sentences using a different conjunction

Questions

a) She wants to go to the party, but she has to study.
b) He prefers tea over coffee.
c) She is tired, and she wants to go to bed.
d) He wants to go to the beach, but it is raining.
e) She wants to go shopping, and she needs new shoes.

Answers

a) She wants to go to the party, although she has to study.
b) He prefers tea to coffee.
c) She is tired, so she wants to go to bed.
d) He wants to go to the beach, however, it is raining.
e) She wants to go shopping, since she needs new shoes.

Exercise 19: Rewrite the sentences using a different conjunction

Questions

a) He ate the sandwich, and he drank the soda.
b) She wants to study abroad, so she is learning a new language.
c) He is tired, but he wants to keep working.
d) She wants to go to the party, but she has to finish her work.
e) She is going to the store, and she needs to buy some milk.

Answers

a) He ate the sandwich, then he drank the soda.
b) She wants to study abroad, therefore, she is learning a new language.

c) He is tired, yet he wants to keep working.

d) She wants to go to the party, although she has to finish her work.

e) She is going to the store, so she needs to buy some milk.

Exercise 20: Rewrite the sentences using a different conjunction

Questions

a) He wants to buy a new car, but he doesn't have enough money.

b) She likes to dance, and she likes to sing.

c) He wants to go to the beach, but it's raining.

d) He can play the guitar, and he can sing.

e) He is going to the gym, and he will be back in an hour.

Answers

a) He wants to buy a new car, however, he doesn't have enough money.

b) She likes to dance, as well as she likes to sing.

c) He wants to go to the beach, yet it's raining.

d) He can play the guitar, as well as he can sing.

e) He is going to the gym, so he will be back in an hour.

Chapter 7: Rewrite the sentence(s) using a different preposition

Exercise 1: Rewrite the sentences using a different preposition

Questions

a) The plane flew over the mountain.
b) The cat hid behind the couch.
c) The plane landed on the runway.
d) The fish swam in the pond.
e) The bird perched on the branch.

Answers

a) The plane flew above the mountain.
b) The cat concealed itself beneath the couch.
c) The plane landed upon the runway.
d) The fish swam within the pond.
e) The bird perched upon the branch.

Exercise 2: Rewrite the sentences using a different preposition

Questions

a) The sun set over the ocean. Rewritten: The sun set across the ocean.
b) The car drove through the tunnel. Rewritten: The car drove via the tunnel.
c) The cat jumped onto the bed. Rewritten: The cat jumped atop the bed.
d) The woman sat next to her husband. Rewritten: The woman sat alongside her husband.
e) The bird flew over the tree. Rewritten: The bird flew above the tree.

Exercise 3: Rewrite the sentences using a different preposition

Questions

a) The dog ran through the field. Rewritten: The dog ran across the field.
b) The cat jumped onto the counter. Rewritten: The cat jumped up onto the counter.
c) The airplane flew over the clouds. Rewritten: The airplane flew above the clouds.
d) The boy climbed onto the roof. Rewritten: The boy climbed up onto the roof.
e) The bird flew under the bridge. Rewritten: The bird flew beneath the bridge.

Exercise 4: Rewrite the sentences using a different preposition

Questions

a) The boy hid behind the tree. Rewritten: The boy concealed himself behind the tree.
b) The boat sailed on the lake. Rewritten: The boat sailed across the lake.
c) The cat jumped off the table. Rewritten: The cat leaped down from the table.
d) The dog ran through the park. Rewritten: The dog ran across the park.
e) The woman walked past the store. Rewritten: The woman walked by the store.

Exercise 5: Rewrite the sentences using a different preposition

Questions

a) The plane flew over the mountains.
b) The cat jumped on the couch.
c) The bird flew into the tree.
d) The cat hid under the bed.
e) The car drove around the block.

Answers

a) The plane flew above the mountains.
b) The cat leaped onto the couch.

c) The bird flew onto the tree.

d) The cat concealed itself beneath the bed.

e) The car drove about the block.

Exercise 6: Rewrite the sentences using a different preposition

Questions

a) The book was on the table.

b) The child sat on the chair.

c) The bird flew over the tree.

d) The cat jumped on the table.

e) The dog ran through the park.

Answers

a) The book was upon the table.

b) The child sat upon the chair.

c) The bird flew above the tree.

d) The cat leaped onto the table.

e) The dog ran across the park.

Exercise 7: Rewrite the sentences using a different preposition

Questions

a) The cat slept in the sun.

b) The bird sat on the branch.

c) The cat ran under the bed.

d) The airplane flew above the clouds.

e) The bird flew over the fence.

Answers

a) The cat slept under the sun.

b) The bird perched upon the branch.

c) The cat ran beneath the bed.

d) The airplane flew over the clouds.

e) The bird flew above the fence.

Exercise 8: Rewrite the sentences using a different preposition

Questions

a) The car drove through the tunnel.

b) The book is on the shelf.

c) The boat sailed on the lake.

d) The train passed through the tunnel.

e) The dog jumped over the fence.

Answers

a) The car drove into the tunnel.

b) The book is atop the shelf.

c) The boat sailed upon the lake.

d) The train passed into the tunnel.

e) The dog leaped above the fence.

Exercise 9: Rewrite the sentences using a different preposition

Questions

a) The bird flew past the tree.

b) The car parked beside the building.

c) The cat jumped on the table.

d) The airplane flew over the mountains.

e) The ball bounced off the wall.

f) The cat hid under the bed.

Answers

a) The bird flew beyond the tree.
b) The car parked adjacent to the building.
c) The cat leapt onto the table.
d) The airplane flew above the mountains.
e) The ball rebounded from the wall.
f) The cat concealed itself beneath the bed.

Exercise 10: Rewrite the sentences using a different preposition

Questions

a) The bird flew above the clouds.
b) The book is on the shelf.
c) The flowers are in the vase.
d) The book is beside the lamp.
e) The phone is on the desk.

Answers

a) The bird soared beyond the clouds.
b) The book is upon the shelf.
c) The flowers are within the vase.
d) The book is adjacent to the lamp.
e) The phone is atop the desk.

Exercise 11: Rewrite the sentences using a different preposition

Questions

a) The painting is behind the couch.
b) The cat is under the table.

c) The book is in the library.

d) The cat is on the roof.

e) The book is on the shelf.

Answers

a) The painting is at the rear of the couch.

b) The cat is beneath the table.

c) The book is inside the library.

d) The cat is atop the roof.

e) The book is upon the shelf.

Exercise 12: Rewrite the sentences using a different preposition

Questions

a) The bird is in the tree.

b) The car is in the garage.

c) The laptop is on the desk.

d) The ball is under the table.

e) The dog is behind the couch.

Answers

a) The bird is perched on the tree.

b) The car is inside the garage.

c) The laptop is atop the desk.

d) The ball is beneath the table.

e) The dog is at the rear of the couch.

Exercise 13: Rewrite the sentences using a different preposition

Questions

a) The ball is next to the chair.

b) The bird is in the cage.

c) The book is on the shelf.

d) The cat climbed up the tree to chase a bird.

e) I am going to the store for some milk.

Answers

a) The ball is beside the chair.

b) The bird is inside the cage.

c) The book is beside the shelf.

d) The cat climbed onto the tree to chase a bird.

e) I am going to the store to buy some milk.

Exercise 14: Rewrite the sentences using a different preposition

Questions

a) The cat slept on the couch.

b) The dog ran around the park.

c) The bird sat on the branch.

d) The flowers grew in the garden.

e) The cat jumped onto the table.

Answers

a) The cat slept beneath the couch.

b) The dog ran through the park.

c) The bird perched atop the branch.

d) The flowers flourished outside the garden.

e) The cat leaped over the table.

Exercise 15: Rewrite the sentences using a different preposition

Questions

a) The book is under the bed.
b) The ball is inside the box.
c) The vase is on the table.
d) The cat walked under the table.
e) The cat sat beside the window.

Answers

a) The book is below the bed.
b) The ball is within the box.
c) The vase sits upon the table.
d) The cat walked beneath the table.
e) The cat sat next to the window.

Exercise 16: Rewrite the sentences using a different preposition

Questions

a) The bird perched on the branch.
b) The ball rolled down the hill.
c) The book is on the shelf.
d) The boat sailed across the lake.
e) The cat jumped on the bed.

Answers

a) The bird sat atop the branch.
b) The ball tumbled down the hill.
c) The book rests upon the shelf.
d) The boat sailed over the lake.
e) The cat leaped onto the bed.

Exercise 17: Rewrite the sentences using a different preposition

Questions

a) The spider crawled on the wall.
b) The plane flew over the ocean.
c) The bird flew through the window.
d) The boy climbed up the tree.
e) The car drove along the highway.

Answers

a) The spider crept up the wall.
b) The plane flew above the ocean.
c) The bird flew into the window.
d) The boy ascended the tree.
e) The car drove across the highway.

Exercise 18: Rewrite the sentences using a different preposition

Questions

a) The cat jumped off the bed.
b) The ball bounced off the wall.
c) The book is on the shelf.
d) The cat jumped on the table.
e) The plane flew under the clouds.

Answers

a) The cat leaped from the bed.
b) The ball rebounded from the wall.
c) The book is atop the shelf.
d) The cat leaped onto the table.

e) The plane flew beneath the clouds.

Exercise 19: Rewrite the sentences using a different preposition

Questions

a) The dog slept under the bed.
b) The bird flew over the fence.
c) The cat sat on the windowsill.
d) The ball rolled under the couch.
e) The bird flew through the window.

Answers

a) The dog slept beneath the bed.
b) The bird soared above the fence.
c) The cat perched on the windowsill.
d) The ball rolled beneath the couch.
e) The bird flew into the window.

Exercise 20: Rewrite the sentences using a different preposition

Questions

a) The book is next to the lamp.
b) The cat jumped off the table.
c) The car drove on the highway.
d) The cat walked on the roof.

Answers

a) The book is beside the lamp.
b) The cat leaped from the table.
c) The car drove along the highway.

d) The cat walked atop the roof.

Chapter 8: Rewrite the sentence(s) using a different modal verb

Exercise 1: Rewrite the sentences using a different modal verb

Questions

a) You must finish your homework before you can watch TV.
b) You must finish your work on time.

Answers

a) You ought to finish your work on time.
b) You should finish your homework before you watch TV.

Chapter 9: Rewrite the sentence(s) using a different noun

Exercise 1: Rewrite the sentences using a different noun

Questions

a) The company announced a new product launch.
b) The teacher handed out the assignments to the students.

Answers

a) The corporation announced a new product launch.
b) The instructor distributed the assignments to the pupils.

Chapter 10: Rewrite the following sentence(s) using an exclamatory sentence

Exercise 1: Rewrite the following sentences using an exclamatory sentence

Question

a) I am so excited to go on vacation!

Answer

a) How excited I am to go on vacation!

Chapter 11: Rewrite the sentence(s) using a different noun form

Exercise 1: Rewrite the sentences using a different noun form

Questions

a) He has a passion for music.
b) He has a love for nature.
c) She has a dislike for spicy food.
d) He has a hatred for injustice.
e) He has an interest in science.

Answers

a) He is passionate about music.
b) He is in love with nature.
c) She dislikes spicy food.
d) He hates injustice.
e) He is interested in science.

Exercise 2: Rewrite the sentences using a different noun form

Questions

a) She has a fear of heights.
b) He has a love for photography.
c) He has a preference for tea over coffee.
d) She has a love for animals.
e) He has a fear of public speaking.

Answers

a) She is afraid of heights.
b) He loves photography.

c) He prefers tea to coffee.

d) She loves animals.

e) He is afraid of public speaking.

Exercise 3: Rewrite the sentences using a different noun form

Questions

a) She has a love for music.

b) He has a passion for cooking.

c) She has a love for reading.

d) He has a fear of the dark.

e) She has a love for travel.

Answers

a) She loves music.

b) He is passionate about cooking.

c) She loves to read.

d) He is afraid of the dark.

e) She loves to travel.

Exercise 4: Rewrite the sentences using a different noun form

Questions

a) He has an interest in photography.

b) She has a fear of heights.

c) He has an obsession with cleanliness.

d) She has an interest in learning new languages.

e) He has a love for music.

Answers

a) He is interested in photography.

b) She is afraid of heights.

c) He is obsessed with cleanliness.

d) She is interested in learning new languages.

e) He loves music.

Exercise 5: Rewrite the sentences using a different noun form

Questions

a) She has a fear of public speaking.

b) He has a passion for cooking.

c) She has a talent for writing.

d) She has a talent for playing the piano.

e) He has a talent for singing.

Answers

a) She is afraid of public speaking.

b) He is passionate about cooking.

c) She is talented at writing.

d) She is talented at playing the piano.

e) He is talented at singing.

Exercise 6: Rewrite the sentences using a different noun form

Questions

a) He has a fear of heights.

b) She has an interest in art.

c) She has a desire to travel the world.

d) He has a passion for photography.

e) She has a love for animals.

Answers

a) He is afraid of heights.
b) She is interested in art.
c) She desires to travel the world.
d) He is passionate about photography.
e) She loves animals.

Exercise 7: Rewrite the sentences using a different noun form

Questions

a) He has an interest in science.
b) She has a preference for chocolate ice cream.
c) She has a talent for playing the piano.
d) He has a fascination with ancient history.
e) She has a fear of heights.

Answers

a) He is interested in science.
b) She prefers chocolate ice cream.
c) She is talented at playing the piano.
d) He is fascinated by ancient history.
e) She is afraid of heights.

Exercise 8: Rewrite the sentences using a different noun form

Questions

a) He has a dislike for spicy food.
b) She has a passion for cooking.
c) He has an understanding of art.
d) She has a desire to travel.

e) He has an interest in music.

Answers

a) He dislikes spicy food.
b) She is passionate about cooking.
c) He understands art.
d) She desires to travel.
e) He is interested in music.

Exercise 9: Rewrite the sentences using a different noun form

Questions

a) He has a hatred for spiders.
b) She has a talent for singing.
c) He has a fear of heights.
d) She has an obsession with cleanliness.
e) He has an appreciation for music.

Answers

a) He hates spiders.
b) She is talented at singing.
c) He is afraid of heights.
d) She is obsessed with cleanliness.
e) He appreciates music.

Exercise 10: Rewrite the sentences using a different noun form

a) She has an interest in photography.
b) He has a love of books.
c) She has a fear of public speaking.
d) He has a talent for drawing.

e) She has a dislike for broccoli.

Answers

a) She is interested in photography.
b) He loves books.
c) She is afraid of public speaking.
d) He is talented at drawing.
e) She dislikes broccoli.

Exercise 11: Rewrite the sentences using a different noun form

Questions

a) He has an aversion to spiders.
b) She has a preference for tea over coffee.
c) He has a desire to travel the world.
d) She has a tendency to procrastinate.
e) He has a passion for music.

Answers

a) He is averse to spiders.
b) She prefers tea over coffee.
c) He desires to travel the world.
d) She tends to procrastinate.
e) He is passionate about music.

Exercise 12: Rewrite the sentences using a different noun form

Questions

a) She has a fear of heights.
b) He has a love for nature.

c) He has a hatred for injustice.

d) She has a love for animals.

e) He has a talent for singing.

Answers

a) She fears heights.

b) He loves nature.

c) He hates injustice.

d) She loves animals.

e) He is talented at singing.

Exercise 13: Rewrite the sentences using a different noun form

Questions

a) He has a fear of spiders.

b) She has a dislike for spicy food.

c) He has a preference for tea over coffee.

d) He has an interest in history.

e) He has a talent for drawing.

Answers

a) He is afraid of spiders.

b) She dislikes spicy food.

c) He prefers tea over coffee.

d) He is interested in history.

e) He is talented at drawing.

Exercise 14: Rewrite the sentences using a different noun form

Questions

a) She has a love for music.

b) He has an appreciation for art.

c) She has a fear of spiders.

d) He has a fear of heights.

e) She has an interest in science.

Answers

a) She loves music.

b) He appreciates art.

c) She fears spiders.

d) He is afraid of heights.

e) She is interested in science.

Exercise 15: Rewrite the sentences using a different noun form

Questions

a) He has a love for photography.

b) She has a passion for cooking.

c) He has a talent for music.

d) She has an appreciation for art.

e) He has a talent for writing.

Answers

a) He loves photography.

b) She is passionate about cooking.

c) He is talented in music.

d) She appreciates art.

e) He is talented at writing.

Exercise 16: Rewrite the sentences using a different noun form

Questions

    a) She has a fear of heights.

    b) He has an interest in history.

    c) He has a love for animals.

    d) He has a preference for tea over coffee.

    e) He has a desire to travel.

Answers

    a) She is afraid of heights.

    b) He is interested in history.

    c) He loves animals.

    d) He prefers tea over coffee.

    e) He desires to travel.

Exercise 17: Rewrite the sentences using a different noun form

Questions

    a) She has a fondness for chocolate.

    b) He has a fear of heights.

    c) She has a talent for singing.

    d) He has an interest in history.

    e) She has a talent for dancing.

Answers

    a) She is fond of chocolate.

    b) He is afraid of heights.

    c) She is talented at singing.

    d) He is interested in history.

    e) She is talented at dancing.

Exercise 18: Rewrite the sentences using a different noun form

Questions

a) He has a fear of spiders.

b) She has a love for animals.

c) He has a love for cooking.

d) She has an interest in fashion.

e) She has a dislike for public speaking.

Answers

a) He is afraid of spiders.

b) She loves animals.

c) He loves to cook.

d) She is interested in fashion.

e) She dislikes public speaking.

Exercise 19: Rewrite the sentences using a different noun form

Questions

a) He has a passion for music.

b) She has a fear of heights.

c) He has a talent for writing.

d) She has a talent for cooking.

e) He has a love for animals.

Answers

a) He is passionate about music.

b) She is afraid of heights.

c) He is talented in writing.

d) She is talented at cooking.

e) He loves animals.

Exercise 20: Rewrite the sentences using a different noun form

Questions

a) He has a fear of public speaking.
b) She has an interest in photography.
c) His favorite hobby is playing video games.
d) She has a fear of spiders.

Answers

a) He is afraid of public speaking.
b) She is interested in photography.
c) He enjoys playing video games as his favorite pastime.
d) She suffers from arachnophobia.

Chapter 12: Rewrite the sentence(s) using a different adverb

Exercise 1: Rewrite the sentences using a different adverb

Questions

a) He walked quickly to catch the bus.
b) She spoke loudly to the audience.
c) He ran quickly to catch the train.
d) She sang beautifully at the concert.
e) He drove carefully on the icy road.

Answers

a) He walked briskly to catch the bus.
b) She spoke boldly to the audience.
c) He ran swiftly to catch the train.
d) She sang magnificently at the concert.
e) He drove cautiously on the icy road.

Exercise 2: Rewrite the sentences using a different adverb

Questions

a) He spoke softly to the baby.
b) She typed quickly on the keyboard.
c) He waited patiently for the bus.
d) He spoke angrily to his boss.
e) She walked slowly down the street.

Answer

a) He spoke gently to the baby.
b) She typed swiftly on the keyboard.

c) He waited calmly for the bus.

d) He spoke furiously to his boss.

e) She walked leisurely down the street.

Exercise 3: Rewrite the sentences using a different adverb

Questions

a) He spoke quietly to his friend.

b) She danced gracefully on stage.

c) The car drove smoothly on the highway.

d) The dog barked loudly at the stranger.

e) She sang beautifully at the concert.

Answers

a) He spoke softly to his friend.

b) She danced elegantly on stage.

c) The car drove seamlessly on the highway.

d) The dog barked boisterously at the stranger.

e) She sang splendidly at the concert.

Exercise 4: Rewrite the sentences using a different adverb

Questions

a) She sang loudly in the shower.

b) The woman walked quickly to catch the bus.

c) The bird flew quickly through the sky.

d) She spoke softly to the baby.

e) The man walked slowly down the street.

Answers

a) She sang boisterously in the shower.

b) The woman walked briskly to catch the bus.

c) The bird flew swiftly through the sky.

d) She spoke gently to the baby.

e) The man walked leisurely down the street.

Exercise 5: Rewrite the sentences using a different adverb

Questions

a) The man spoke loudly in the restaurant.

b) The girl smiled happily at her parents.

c) The man walked quietly down the hall.

d) The woman spoke loudly to her friend.

e) The man sang beautifully on stage.

Answers

a) The man spoke vociferously in the restaurant.

b) The girl smiled joyfully at her parents.

c) The man walked silently down the hall.

d) The woman spoke boldly to her friend.

e) The man sang melodiously on stage.

Exercise 6: Rewrite the sentences using a different adverb

Questions

a) The woman drove cautiously on the icy road.

b) The man walked quickly to catch the bus.

c) The woman spoke softly to her baby.

d) The man drove carefully on the icy road.

e) The man spoke softly to his wife.

Answers

a) The woman drove prudently on the icy road.

b) The man walked briskly to catch the bus.

c) The woman spoke gently to her baby.

d) The man drove cautiously on the icy road.

e) The man spoke tenderly to his wife.

Exercise 7: Rewrite the sentences using a different adverb

Questions

a) The woman walked quickly to catch the train.

b) The man spoke loudly to his friend.

c) The woman smiled happily at her children.

d) The man worked hard on the project.

e) The woman sang beautifully at the concert.

Answers

a) The woman walked swiftly to catch the train.

b) The man spoke boisterously to his friend.

c) The woman smiled joyfully at her children.

d) The man worked diligently on the project.

e) The woman sang melodiously at the concert.

Exercise 8: Rewrite the sentences using a different adverb

Questions

a) The man spoke confidently during his presentation.

b) The woman walked slowly down the street.

c) The man drove carefully on the icy road.

d) The woman spoke softly to her child.

e) The man walked quickly to catch the train.

Answers

a) The man spoke assuredly during his presentation.
b) The woman walked leisurely down the street.
c) The man drove cautiously on the icy road.
d) The woman spoke quietly to her child.
e) The man walked swiftly to catch the train.

Exercise 9: Rewrite the sentences using a different adverb

Questions

a) The child ran quickly to catch up with his friends.
b) The man spoke loudly during the meeting.
c) The woman spoke clearly during the presentation.
d) The man drove slowly on the winding road.
e) The dog barked loudly at the mailman.

Answers

a) The child ran rapidly to catch up with his friends.
b) The man spoke boisterously during the meeting.
c) The woman spoke distinctly during the presentation.
d) The man drove cautiously on the winding road.
e) The dog barked noisily at the mailman.

Exercise 10: Rewrite the sentences using a different adverb

Questions

a) The child cried loudly when she fell.
b) The woman sang beautifully at the concert.

c) The man walked slowly down the street.

d) The woman spoke softly to the baby.

e) The man drove carefully on the icy road.

Answers

a) The child cried vehemently when she fell.

b) The woman sang melodiously at the concert.

c) The man walked leisurely down the street.

d) The woman spoke tenderly to the baby.

e) The man drove cautiously on the icy road.

Exercise 11: Rewrite the sentences using a different adverb

Questions

a) The child laughed happily at the clown.

b) The man spoke quietly to his wife.

c) The woman walked quickly to catch the bus.

d) The boy ran quickly to the finish line.

e) The child spoke loudly to get attention.

Answers

a) The child laughed joyfully at the clown.

b) The man spoke softly to his wife.

c) The woman walked swiftly to catch the bus.

d) The boy ran speedily to the finish line.

e) The child spoke boldly to get attention.

Exercise 12: Rewrite the sentences using a different adverb

Questions

a) The man spoke politely to the customer.

b) The man drove carefully on the icy road.

c) The woman smiled warmly at the child.

d) The child laughed happily at the joke.

e) The woman spoke softly to the baby.

Answers

a) The man spoke courteously to the customer.

b) The man drove cautiously on the icy road.

c) The woman smiled kindly at the child.

d) The child laughed gleefully at the joke.

e) The woman spoke gently to the baby.

Exercise 13: Rewrite the sentences using a different adverb

Questions

a) The man walked slowly down the street.

b) The woman ran quickly to catch the bus.

c) The baby cried loudly in the movie theater.

d) The man spoke quietly during the meeting.

e) The boy walked slowly to the store.

Answers

a) The man walked leisurely down the street.

b) The woman ran swiftly to catch the bus.

c) The baby cried noisily in the movie theater.

d) The man spoke softly during the meeting.

e) The boy walked leisurely to the store.

Exercise 14: Rewrite the sentences using a different adverb

Questions

a) The woman spoke softly to the baby.

b) The man drove cautiously on the icy road.

c) The woman sang beautifully in the choir.

d) The child ran quickly to the playground.

e) The woman spoke loudly to the crowd.

Answers

a) The woman spoke quietly to the baby.

b) The man drove prudently on the icy road.

c) The woman sang melodiously in the choir.

d) The child ran rapidly to the playground.

e) The woman spoke vociferously to the crowd.

Exercise 15: Rewrite the sentences using a different adverb

Questions

a) The man drove recklessly on the highway.

b) The woman spoke softly to the baby.

c) The man spoke quietly to the woman.

d) The woman walked slowly to the store.

e) The man walked quickly to catch the bus.

Answers

a) The man drove carelessly on the highway.

b) The woman spoke gently to the baby.

c) The man spoke softly to the woman.

d) The woman walked leisurely to the store.

e) The man walked swiftly to catch the bus.

Exercise 16: Rewrite the sentences using a different adverb

Questions

a) The woman sings beautifully.

b) The man worked diligently on the project.

c) The woman spoke softly to the child.

d) The man spoke loudly to the crowd.

e) The boy runs quickly.

Answers

a) The woman sings superbly.

b) The man worked assiduously on the project.

c) The woman spoke gently to the child.

d) The man spoke boisterously to the crowd.

e) The boy runs swiftly.

Exercise 17: Rewrite the sentences using a different adverb

Questions

a) The girl sings beautifully.

b) She sang beautifully at the concert last night.

c) He spoke confidently in front of the audience.

d) He ate his dinner quickly.

e) She spoke softly to the baby.

Answers

a) The girl sings splendidly.

b) She sang wonderfully at the concert last night.

c) He spoke boldly in front of the audience.

d) He ate his dinner hastily.

e) She spoke gently to the baby.

Exercise 18: Rewrite the sentences using a different adverb

Questions

a) He waited patiently for her to arrive.

b) He spoke loudly to get their attention.

c) She laughed happily at the joke.

d) He walked slowly down the street.

e) She smiled warmly at the child.

Answers

a) He waited eagerly for her to arrive.

b) He spoke boldly to get their attention.

c) She laughed heartily at the joke.

d) He walked sluggishly down the street.

e) She smiled kindly at the child.

Exercise 19: Rewrite the sentences using a different adverb

Questions

a) He typed quickly on the keyboard.

b) She sang beautifully in the concert.

c) He drove carefully on the icy road.

d) She danced gracefully on stage.

e) He spoke softly to the baby.

Answers

a) He typed rapidly on the keyboard.

b) She sang exquisitely in the concert.

c) He drove cautiously on the icy road.

d) She danced elegantly on stage.

e) He spoke gently to the baby.

Exercise 20: Rewrite the sentences using a different adverb

Questions

a) He walked quietly through the library.

b) She laughed happily at the joke.

c) He walked slowly down the street.

d) He worked hard on the project.

e) He drove cautiously on the icy road.

Answers

a) He walked stealthily through the library.

b) She laughed joyfully at the joke.

c) He walked leisurely down the street.

d) He worked diligently on the project.

e) He drove prudently on the icy road.

Chapter 13: Rewrite the sentence(s) using a different adjective

Exercise 1: Rewrite the sentences using a different adjective

Questions

   a) The movie was scary.
   b) The book was interesting.
   c) The sunset was beautiful.
   d) The weather was hot.
   e) The shirt was red.

Answers

   a) The movie was frightening.
   b) The book was captivating.
   c) The sunset was gorgeous.
   d) The weather was scorching.
   e) The shirt was crimson.

Exercise 2: Rewrite the sentences using a different adjective

Questions

   a) The movie was sad.
   b) The house was big.
   c) The concert was loud.
   d) The dog was cute.
   e) The coffee was hot.

Answers

   a) The movie was melancholy.
   b) The house was spacious.

c) The concert was boisterous.

d) The dog was adorable.

e) The coffee was steaming.

Exercise 3: Rewrite the sentences using a different adjective

Questions

a) The book was interesting.

b) The weather was cold.

c) The car was fast.

d) The movie was scary.

e) The book was sad.

Answers

a) The book was captivating.

b) The weather was frigid.

c) The car was speedy.

d) The movie was frightening.

e) The book was heartbreaking.

Exercise 4: Rewrite the sentences using a different adjective

Questions

a) The baby was cute.

b) The sunset was beautiful.

c) The weather was hot.

d) The beach was crowded.

e) The music was loud.

Answers

a) The baby was adorable.

b) The sunset was stunning.

c) The weather was scorching.

d) The beach was packed.

e) The music was deafening.

Exercise 5: Rewrite the sentences using a different adjective

Questions

a) The plant was tall.

b) The movie was scary.

c) The book was interesting.

d) The car was fast.

e) The flowers were pretty.

Answers

a) The plant was towering.

b) The movie was terrifying.

c) The book was captivating.

d) The car was rapid.

e) The flowers were beautiful.

Exercise 6: Rewrite the sentences using a different adjective

Questions

a) The beach was crowded.

b) The music was loud.

c) The house was old.

d) The movie was funny.

e) The sunset was beautiful.

Answers

a) The beach was congested.

b) The music was boisterous.

c) The house was ancient.

d) The movie was hilarious.

e) The sunset was breathtaking.

Exercise 7: Rewrite the sentences using a different adjective

Questions

a) The park was peaceful.

b) The book was interesting.

c) The party was fun.

d) The beach was hot.

e) The mountain was high.

Answers

a) The park was serene.

b) The book was captivating.

c) The party was enjoyable.

d) The beach was scorching.

e) The mountain was towering.

Exercise 8: Rewrite the sentences using a different adjective

Questions

a) The movie was scary.

b) The flower was pretty.

c) The party was crowded.

d) The sky was blue.

e) The girl was happy.

Answers

a) The movie was chilling.
b) The flower was beautiful.
c) The party was packed.
d) The sky was azure.
e) The girl was ecstatic.

Exercise 9: Rewrite the sentences using a different adjective

Questions

a) The coffee was bitter.
b) The beach was beautiful.
c) The movie was scary.
d) The flower was beautiful.
e) The dress was red.

Answers

a) The coffee was acrid.
b) The beach was picturesque.
c) The movie was frightening.
d) The flower was stunning.
e) The dress was scarlet.

Exercise 10: Rewrite the sentences using a different adjective

Questions

a) The day was hot.
b) The music was loud.

c) The water was cold.

d) The sunset was beautiful.

e) The movie was scary.

Answers

a) The day was scorching.

b) The music was deafening.

c) The water was frigid.

d) The sunset was breathtaking.

e) The movie was terrifying.

Exercise 11: Rewrite the sentences using a different adjective

Questions

a) The dog was friendly.

b) The house was old.

c) The weather was hot.

d) The food was spicy.

e) The book was boring.

Answers

a) The dog was amiable.

b) The house was ancient.

c) The weather was sweltering.

d) The food was piquant.

e) The book was tedious.

Exercise 12: Rewrite the sentences using a different adjective

Questions

a) The movie was scary.

b) The movie was funny.

c) The game was boring.

d) The weather was hot.

e) The cake was delicious.

Answers

a) The movie was frightening.

b) The movie was amusing.

c) The game was uninteresting.

d) The weather was scorching.

e) The cake was delectable.

Exercise 13: Rewrite the sentences using a different adjective

Questions

a) The dog was cute.

b) The painting was beautiful.

c) The movie was scary.

d) The book was interesting.

e) The weather was hot.

Answers

a) The dog was adorable.

b) The painting was exquisite.

c) The movie was frightening.

d) The book was captivating.

e) The weather was scorching.

Exercise 14: Rewrite the sentences using a different adjective

Questions

a) The room was messy.
b) The old man walked slowly down the street.
c) The sky was blue and cloudless.
d) The food at the restaurant was delicious.
e) The movie was scary.

Answers

a) The room was disorganized.
b) The elderly man walked leisurely down the street.
c) The sky was azure and cloudless.
d) The food at the restaurant was scrumptious.
e) The movie was terrifying.

Exercise 15: Rewrite the sentences using a different adjective

Questions

a) The book was interesting.
b) The party was fun.
c) The cake was sweet.
d) The sunset was beautiful.
e) The sunset was stunning.

Answers

a) The book was captivating.
b) The party was enjoyable.
c) The cake was sugary.
d) The sunset was picturesque.
e) The sunset was breathtaking.

Exercise 16: Rewrite the sentences using a different adjective

Questions

   a) The party was loud.
   b) The weather was hot.
   c) The movie was sad.
   d) The book was boring.
   e) The music was loud.

Answers

   a) The party was raucous.
   b) The weather was sweltering.
   c) The movie was melancholic.
   d) The book was tedious.
   e) The music was deafening.

Exercise 17: Rewrite the sentences using a different adjective

Questions

   a) The sky was blue.
   b) The painting was beautiful.
   c) The house was old.
   d) The movie was scary.
   e) The food was spicy.

Answers

   a) The sky was azure.
   b) The painting was exquisite.
   c) The house was ancient.
   d) The movie was terrifying.

e) The food was piquant.

Exercise 18: Rewrite the sentences using a different adjective

Questions

a) The weather was hot.
b) The beach was crowded.
c) The meal was delicious.
d) The movie was boring.
e) The sunset was beautiful.

Answers

a) The weather was scorching.
b) The beach was packed.
c) The meal was delectable.
d) The movie was dull.
e) The sunset was stunning.

Exercise 19: Rewrite the sentences using a different adjective

Questions

a) The building was tall.
b) The dog was cute.
c) The sky was blue.
d) The flower was pretty.
e) The dress was beautiful.

Answers

a) The building was lofty.
b) The dog was adorable.

c) The sky was azure.

d) The flower was lovely.

e) The dress was stunning.

Exercise 20: Rewrite the sentences using a different adjective

Questions

a) The city was noisy.

b) The food was spicy.

c) The music was loud.

d) The sunset was beautiful.

Answers

a) The city was cacophonous.

b) The food was piquant.

c) The music was deafening.

d) The sunset was stunning.

Chapter 14: Rewrite the sentence(s) using a different verb

Exercise 1: Rewrite the sentences using a different verb

Questions

a) The woman walked her dog.
b) The children played with the ball.
c) The girl sang a song.
d) The boy ate his breakfast.
e) The girl wrote a letter.

Answers

a) The woman strolled with her dog.
b) The children frolicked with the ball.
c) The girl performed a song.
d) The boy devoured his breakfast.
e) The girl penned a letter.

Exercise 2: Rewrite the sentences using a different verb

Questions

a) The man drove his car.
b) The children watched TV.
c) The cat slept on the couch.
d) The woman cooked dinner.
e) The man jogged in the park.

Answers

a) The man operated his car.
b) The children viewed TV.

c) The cat dozed on the couch.

d) The woman prepared dinner.

e) The man ran in the park.

Exercise 3: Rewrite the sentences using a different verb

Questions

a) The girl danced in the ballet.

b) The child drew a picture.

c) The boy ate a sandwich.

d) The man drank a glass of water.

e) The boy played with his toy cars.

Answers

a) The girl performed in the ballet.

b) The child sketched a picture.

c) The boy consumed a sandwich.

d) The man sipped a glass of water.

e) The boy toyed with his toy cars.

Exercise 4: Rewrite the sentences using a different verb

Questions

a) The woman drank a cup of tea.

b) The man wrote a letter.

c) The woman baked a cake.

d) The girl danced in the recital.

e) The dog barked at the mailman.

Answers

a) The woman sipped a cup of tea.

b) The man penned a letter.

c) The woman cooked a cake.

d) The girl performed in the recital.

e) The dog growled at the mailman.

Exercise 5: Rewrite the sentences using a different verb

Questions

a) The child ate a cookie.

b) The boy kicked the ball.

c) The man sang a song.

d) The child ran to catch the ball.

e) The man cooked dinner for his family.

Answers

a) The child devoured a cookie.

b) The boy struck the ball.

c) The man performed a song.

d) The child sprinted to catch the ball.

e) The man prepared dinner for his family.

Exercise 6: Rewrite the sentences using a different verb

Questions

a) The woman wrote a letter.

b) The man played the guitar.

c) The woman took a photograph.

d) The boy caught the ball.

e) The child ate breakfast.

Answers

a) The woman composed a letter.

b) The man strummed the guitar.

c) The woman captured a photograph.

d) The boy snagged the ball.

e) The child consumed breakfast.

Exercise 7: Rewrite the sentences using a different verb

Questions

a) The woman drank water.

b) The man wrote a poem.

c) The man bought a car.

d) The woman cooked dinner.

e) The man took a photograph.

Answers

a) The woman imbibed water.

b) The man composed a poem.

c) The man purchased a car.

d) The woman prepared dinner.

e) The man snapped a photograph.

Exercise 8: Rewrite the sentences using a different verb

Questions

a) The woman danced at the party.

b) The man played the guitar.

c) The woman drank a cup of coffee.

d) The man wrote a letter.

e) The man ate breakfast.

Answers

a) The woman grooved at the party.
b) The man strummed the guitar.
c) The woman sipped a cup of coffee.
d) The man composed a letter.
e) The man consumed breakfast.

Exercise 9: Rewrite the sentences using a different verb

Questions

a) The man ran a marathon.
b) The woman read a book.
c) The child played with her toys.
d) The man played the guitar.
e) The woman drank a glass of water.

Answers

a) The man completed a marathon.
b) The woman perused a book.
c) The child entertained herself with her toys.
d) The man strummed the guitar.
e) The woman consumed a glass of water.

Exercise 10: Rewrite the sentences using a different verb

Questions

a) The man watched TV.
b) The boy ate an apple.

c) The girl sang a song.

d) The man drove to work.

e) The boy kicked the ball.

Answers

a) The man viewed TV.

b) The boy consumed an apple.

c) The girl performed a song.

d) The man commuted to work.

e) The boy struck the ball.

Exercise 11: Rewrite the sentences using a different verb

Questions

a) The girl danced in the recital.

b) The man jogged around the park.

c) The woman typed an email.

d) The child drew a picture.

e) The woman walked the dog.

Answers

a) The girl performed in the recital.

b) The man ran around the park.

c) The woman composed an email.

d) The child sketched a picture.

e) The woman strolled with the dog.

Exercise 12: Rewrite the sentences using a different verb

Questions

a) The man drove the car.

b) The child ate the candy.

c) The man read the newspaper.

d) The woman cooked dinner.

e) The man sang a song.

Answers

a) The man operated the car.

b) The child consumed the candy.

c) The man perused the newspaper.

d) The woman prepared dinner.

e) The man performed a song.

Exercise 13: Rewrite the sentences using a different verb

Questions

a) The woman cleaned the house.

b) The man played the guitar.

c) The children played in the park.

d) The students studied for the test.

e) The boy rode his bike to school.

Answers

a) The woman tidied the house.

b) The man strummed the guitar.

c) The children frolicked in the park.

d) The students prepared for the test.

e) The boy cycled to school.

Exercise 14: Rewrite the sentences using a different verb

Questions

a) The woman cooked dinner for her family.
b) The man walked to the store.
c) The dog barked loudly at the mailman.
d) The kids played in the park all day.
e) The bird flew across the sky.

Answers

a) The woman prepared dinner for her family.
b) The man strolled to the store.
c) The dog growled fiercely at the mailman.
d) The children frolicked in the park all day.
e) The bird soared across the sky.

Exercise 15: Rewrite the sentences using a different verb

Questions

a) The car drove down the road.
b) The boy ran to catch the ball.
c) The bird sang a beautiful song.
d) The kids laughed and played in the park.
e) The cat meowed loudly.

Answers

a) The car cruised down the road.
b) The boy sprinted to catch the ball.
c) The bird chirped a beautiful song.
d) The children giggled and played in the park.
e) The cat yowled loudly.

Exercise 16: Rewrite the sentences using a different verb

Questions

a) The dog barked at the mailman.
b) The baby cried all night.
c) The wind blew the leaves off the tree.
d) The bell rang loudly.
e) The car honked at the pedestrian.

Answers

a) The dog howled at the mailman.
b) The baby wailed all night.
c) The wind rustled the leaves off the tree.
d) The bell chimed loudly.
e) The car beeped at the pedestrian.

Exercise 17: Rewrite the sentences using a different verb

Questions

a) The children played in the park.
b) The cat scratched the couch.
c) The baby slept in the crib.
d) The flowers bloomed in the spring.
e) The dog barked at the mailman.

Answers

a) The children frolicked in the park.
b) The cat clawed the couch.
c) The baby dozed in the crib.

d) The flowers blossomed in the spring.

e) The dog yapped at the mailman.

Exercise 18: Rewrite the sentences using a different verb

Questions

a) The child giggled at the joke.

b) The car skidded on the wet road.

c) The children played with their toys.

d) The bird chirped in the tree.

e) The woman jogged in the park.

Answers

a) The child chuckled at the joke.

b) The car slid on the wet road.

c) The children frolicked with their toys.

d) The bird twittered in the tree.

e) The woman ran in the park.

Exercise 19: Rewrite the sentences using a different verb

Questions

a) The boy sprinted down the street.

b) The man smiled at the baby.

c) The child cried when he fell down.

d) The teacher explained the lesson.

e) The boy laughed at the joke.

Answers

a) The boy dashed down the street.

b) The man grinned at the baby.

c) The child wept when he fell down.

d) The teacher elucidated the lesson.

e) The boy chuckled at the joke.

Exercise 20: Rewrite the sentences using a different verb

Questions

a) The man ate his breakfast.

b) The baby crawled on the floor.

c) The man drank a cup of coffee.

Answers

a) The man consumed his breakfast.

b) The baby crept on the floor.

c) The man sipped a cup of coffee.

Chapter 15: Rewrite the sentence(s) using a different pronoun

Exercise 1: Rewrite the sentences using a different pronoun

Questions

a) They went to the store to buy groceries.
b) We went to the park to have a picnic.
c) She gave him a birthday present.
d) They watched the movie together.
e) We went to the museum yesterday.

Answers

a) He went to the store to buy groceries.
b) They went to the park to have a picnic.
c) He received a birthday present from her.
d) She watched the movie with him.
e) They went to the museum yesterday.

Exercise 2: Rewrite the sentences using a different pronoun

Questions

a) He gave her a bouquet of flowers.
b) They visited the museum last weekend.
c) She cooked dinner for him.
d) They cleaned the house together.
e) We took a walk in the park.

Answers

a) She received a bouquet of flowers from him.

b) He visited the museum last weekend.

c) He was cooked dinner by her.

d) She cleaned the house with him.

e) They took a walk in the park.

Exercise 3: Rewrite the sentences using a different pronoun

Questions

a) He bought her a bouquet of roses.

b) They went to the beach together.

c) She gave him a present for his birthday.

d) They went to the movie theater.

e) She called them on the phone.

Answers

a) She received a bouquet of roses from him.

b) He went to the beach with them.

c) He received a present from her for his birthday.

d) She went to the movie theater with them.

e) They were called on the phone by her.

Exercise 4: Rewrite the sentences using a different pronoun

Questions

a) He sent her a message.

b) They gave him a gift for his birthday.

c) She invited him to the party.

d) They left the party early.

e) She baked him a cake.

Answers

a) She received a message from him.

b) He received a gift from them for his birthday.

c) He was invited to the party by her.

d) The party was left early by them.

e) He received a cake baked by her.

Exercise 5: Rewrite the sentences using a different pronoun

Questions

a) They met her at the restaurant.

b) She helped them with the project.

c) He sent them a gift.

d) She gave him a book.

e) They offered her a job.

Answers

a) She was met at the restaurant by them.

b) They received help with the project from her.

c) They received a gift from him.

d) He received a book from her.

e) She was offered a job by them.

Exercise 6: Rewrite the sentences using a different pronoun

Questions

a) She gave them a ride home.

b) He showed her the way to the park.

c) He sent her a message.

d) They told him the news.

e) She baked them a cake.

Answers

a) They received a ride home from her.

b) She was shown the way to the park by him.

c) She received a message from him.

d) He was told the news by them.

e) They received a cake from her.

Exercise 7: Rewrite the sentences using a different pronoun

Questions

a) He taught her how to ride a bike.

b) He sent them a gift.

c) She gave him a present.

d) They told her the truth.

e) He sent them a message.

Answers

a) She learned how to ride a bike from him.

b) They received a gift from him.

c) He received a present from her.

d) She was told the truth by them.

e) They received a message from him.

Exercise 8: Rewrite the sentences using a different pronoun

Questions

a) She showed him the way.

b) They gave her a present.

c) She told him the truth.

d) They gave him a book.

e) He showed her the way.

Answers

a) He was shown the way by her.

b) She received a present from them.

c) He was told the truth by her.

d) He received a book from them.

e) She was shown the way by him.

Exercise 9: Rewrite the sentences using a different pronoun

Questions

a) She bought him a present.

b) They told her the news.

c) He helped her with her homework.

d) They showed him the way.

e) She lent him her book.

Answers

a) He received a present from her.

b) She was told the news by them.

c) She received help with her homework from him.

d) He was shown the way by them.

e) He borrowed her book.

Exercise 10: Rewrite the sentences using a different pronoun

Questions

a) They sent her a gift.

b) He told her the truth.

c) They bought her a present.

d) They sold him the car.

e) She taught them how to swim.

Answers

a) She received a gift from them.

b) She was told the truth by him.

c) She received a present from them.

d) He bought the car from them.

e) They learned how to swim from her.

Exercise 11: Rewrite the sentences using a different pronoun

Questions

a) They offered her a job.

b) He showed her the painting.

c) They sent him a message.

d) She gave them the tickets.

e) He told her the news.

Answers

a) She was offered a job by them.

b) She was shown the painting by him.

c) He received a message from them.

d) They received the tickets from her.

e) She received the news from him.

Exercise 12: Rewrite the sentences using a different pronoun

Questions

a) They showed him the way.

b) She lent him a book.

c) They bought her a gift.

d) He gave her a gift.

e) She gave him a present.

Answers

a) He was shown the way by them.

b) He borrowed a book from her.

c) She received a gift from them.

d) She received a gift from him.

e) He received a present from her.

Exercise 13: Rewrite the sentences using a different pronoun

Questions

a) They gave her a gift.

b) He showed them the way.

c) She sent him a letter.

d) They showed her the way.

e) He bought her a gift.

Answers

a) She received a gift from them.

b) They were shown the way by him.

c) He received a letter from her.

d) She was shown the way by them.

e) She received a gift from him.

Exercise 14: Rewrite the sentences using a different pronoun

Questions

a) They gave him a book.

b) She told them the story.

c) They baked her a cake.

d) He showed her the way.

e) They gave him a present.

Answers

a) He received a book from them.

b) They were told the story by her.

c) She received a cake from them.

d) She was shown the way by him.

e) He received a present from them.

Exercise 15: Rewrite the sentences using a different pronoun

Questions

a) She gave them a gift.

b) They sent her a postcard.

c) He showed them the way.

d) They sent him a postcard.

e) She showed him the way.

Answers

a) They received a gift from her.

b) She received a postcard from them.

c) They were shown the way by him.

d) He received a postcard from them.

e) He was shown the way by her.

Exercise 16: Rewrite the sentences using a different pronoun

Questions

a) They sent us a letter.
b) He gave her a present.
c) She showed us the way.
d) They invited us to the party.
e) He told her a secret.

Answers

a) We received a letter from them.
b) She received a present from him.
c) We were shown the way by her.
d) We were invited to the party by them.
e) She was told a secret by him.

Exercise 17: Rewrite the sentences using a different pronoun

Questions

a) She gave him a gift.
b) He asked her a question.
c) They sent us a gift.
d) She gave them a ride.
e) He showed her his new car.

Answers

a) He received a gift from her.
b) She was asked a question by him.
c) We were sent a gift by them.

d) They were given a ride by her.

e) She was shown his new car by him.

Exercise 18: Rewrite the sentences using a different pronoun

Questions

a) He bought her a necklace.
b) She gave him a book.
c) They gave her a birthday present.
d) He showed them his artwork.
e) She bought him a gift.

Answers

a) She received a necklace from him.
b) He was given a book by her.
c) She received a birthday present from them.
d) They were shown his artwork by him.
e) He received a gift from her.

Exercise 19: Rewrite the sentences using a different pronoun

Questions

a) They told her a secret.
b) He gave her a ride home.
c) They brought him a present.
d) She showed him her artwork.
e) They gave her a hug.

Answers

a) She was told a secret by them.

b) She received a ride home from him.

c) He received a present from them.

d) He was shown her artwork by her.

e) She received a hug from them.

Exercise 20: Rewrite the sentences using a different pronoun

Questions

a) She sent him a letter.

b) They helped her with the project.

c) He gave her the flowers as a present.

Answers

a) He received a letter from her.

b) She received help with the project from them.

c) She gave him the flowers as a present.

Chapter 16: Rewrite the sentence(s) using a different tense

Exercise 1: Rewrite the sentences using a different tense

Questions

a) They will be going on vacation next month.
b) She is going to the gym later.
c) They are going to the beach tomorrow.
d) They have been working on the project for a week.

Answers

a) They have planned to go on vacation next month.
b) She plans to go to the gym later.
c) They will be going to the beach tomorrow.
d) They worked on the project for a week.

Exercise 2: Rewrite the sentences using a different tense

Questions

a) She will have been living here for a year next month.
b) They have already finished their dinner.
c) They will have been married for 10 years next month.
d) They have been friends since they were kids.
e) They will have been living in the city for 5 years next month.

Answers

a) She has been living here for almost a year.
b) They finished their dinner earlier.
c) They have been married for almost 10 years.
d) They were friends since they were kids.

e) They have been living in the city for almost 5 years.

Exercise 3: Rewrite the sentences using a different tense

Questions

a) They will be traveling to Europe next month.
b) They had been studying for the exam for weeks.
c) They will have finished their project by next week.
d) They have been living in the apartment for a year.
e) They will have been married for 20 years next month.

Answers

a) They plan to travel to Europe next month.
b) They studied for the exam for weeks.
c) They will finish their project by next week.
d) They lived in the apartment for a year.
e) They have been married for almost 20 years.

Exercise 4: Rewrite the sentences using a different tense

Questions

a) They had been planning the party for weeks.
b) They will have completed the project by the end of the month.
c) They have been waiting for an hour.
d) They will have graduated from college by next year.
e) They have been living in the city for three years.

Answers

a) They planned the party for weeks.
b) They will complete the project by the end of the month.

c) They waited for an hour.

d) They will graduate from college by next year.

e) They lived in the city for three years.

Exercise 5: Rewrite the sentences using a different tense

Questions

a) They have been dating for two years.

b) They will have finished the project by tomorrow.

c) They have been working on the project for a month.

d) They have been hiking for hours.

e) They will have been married for ten years next month.

Answers

a) They dated for two years.

b) They will finish the project by tomorrow.

c) They worked on the project for a month.

d) They hiked for hours.

e) They will be married for ten years next month.

Exercise 6: Rewrite the sentences using a different tense

Questions

a) They have been friends since childhood.

b) They have been studying for the test for a week.

c) They will have graduated from college next month.

d) They have been waiting for the bus for half an hour.

e) They have been walking for an hour.

Questions

a) They were friends since childhood.

b) They studied for the test for a week.

c) They will graduate from college next month.

d) They waited for the bus for half an hour.

e) They walked for an hour.

Exercise 7: Rewrite the sentences using a different tense

Questions

a) They will have finished their project by tomorrow.

b) They have been planning the trip for months.

c) They have been living in the city for five years.

d) They will have completed the project by Friday.

e) They have been dating for six months.

Answers

a) They will finish their project by tomorrow.

b) They planned the trip for months.

c) They lived in the city for five years.

d) They will complete the project by Friday.

e) They dated for six months.

Exercise 8: Rewrite the sentences using a different tense

Questions

a) They have been studying for the exam for weeks.

b) They have been living in the apartment for two years.

c) They will have been married for ten years next month.

d) They have been friends for ten years.

e) They have been hiking for hours.

Answers

    a) They studied for the exam for weeks.

    b) They lived in the apartment for two years.

    c) They will be married for ten years next month.

    d) They were friends for ten years.

    e) They hiked for hours.

Exercise 9: Rewrite the sentences using a different tense

Questions

    a) They have been waiting for an hour.

    b) They have been living in this house for five years.

    c) They have been playing soccer for two hours.

    d) They have been studying for the test all week.

    e) They have been working on the project for months.

Answers

    a) They waited for an hour.

    b) They lived in this house for five years.

    c) They played soccer for two hours.

    d) They studied for the test all week.

    e) They worked on the project for months.

Exercise 10: Rewrite the sentences using a different tense

Questions

    a) They have been playing the piano for years.

    b) They have been watching TV all day.

    c) They have been walking for miles.

    d) They have been waiting for hours.

e) They have been cleaning the house all day.

Answers

a) They played the piano for years.
b) They watched TV all day.
c) They walked for miles.
d) They waited for hours.
e) They cleaned the house all day.

Exercise 11: Rewrite the sentences using a different tense

Questions

a) They have been exercising for an hour.
b) They have been studying for the test all week.
c) They have been working on the project for months.
d) They have been planning the party for weeks.
e) They have been living in the city for five years.

Answers

a) They exercised for an hour.
b) They studied for the test all week.
c) They worked on the project for months.
d) They planned the party for weeks.
e) They lived in the city for five years.

Exercise 12: Rewrite the sentences using a different tense

Questions

a) They have been arguing for hours.
b) They have been playing video games all day.

c) They have been talking on the phone for an hour.

d) They have been watching a movie all afternoon.

e) They have been working on the project for weeks.

Answers

a) They argued for hours.

b) They played video games all day.

c) They talked on the phone for an hour.

d) They watched a movie all afternoon.

e) They worked on the project for weeks.

Exercise 13: Rewrite the sentences using a different tense

Questions

a) They have been studying for the exam for days.

b) They have been walking for miles.

c) They have been waiting for hours.

d) They have been playing soccer all afternoon.

e) They have been practicing for the performance for weeks.

Answers

a) They studied for the exam for days.

b) They walked for miles.

c) They waited for hours.

d) They played soccer all afternoon.

e) They practiced for the performance for weeks.

Exercise 14: Rewrite the sentences using a different tense

Questions

a) They have been hiking for hours.

b) They have been cleaning the house all day.

c) They have been studying for the test for weeks.

d) They have been hiking in the mountains all day.

e) They have been waiting for the bus for an hour.

Answers

a) They hiked for hours.

b) They cleaned the house all day.

c) They studied for the test for weeks.

d) They hiked in the mountains all day.

e) They waited for the bus for an hour.

Exercise 15: Rewrite the sentences using a different tense

Questions

a) They have been playing tennis all afternoon.

b) They have been working on the project for months.

c) They have been studying Spanish for years.

d) They have been watching TV all day.

e) They have been cleaning the house all morning.

Answers

a) They played tennis all afternoon.

b) They worked on the project for months.

c) They studied Spanish for years.

d) They watched TV all day.

e) They cleaned the house all morning.

Exercise 16: Rewrite the sentences using a different tense

Questions

a) They have been planning the trip for weeks.

b) They have been waiting for an hour.

c) They have been living in this house for five years.

d) They have been working together for a year.

e) They have been studying for the test all week.

Answers

a) They planned the trip for weeks.

b) They waited for an hour.

c) They lived in this house for five years.

d) They worked together for a year.

e) They studied for the test all week.

Exercise 17: Rewrite the sentences using a different tense

Questions

a) They have been dating for three months.

b) They have been running for an hour.

c) They have been waiting for an hour.

d) They have been watching a movie for two hours.

e) They have been hiking for three hours.

Answers

a) They dated for three months.

b) They ran for an hour.

c) They waited for an hour.

d) They watched a movie for two hours.

e) They hiked for three hours.

Exercise 18: Rewrite the sentences using a different tense

Questions

    a) They have been practicing for the concert.

    b) They have been talking for hours.

    c) They have been playing tennis all morning.

    d) They have been walking for miles.

    e) They have been studying for the exam.

Answers

    a) They practiced for the concert.

    b) They talked for hours.

    c) They played tennis all morning.

    d) They walked for miles.

    e) They studied for the exam.

Exercise 19: Rewrite the sentences using a different tense

Questions

    a) They have been working on the project for weeks.

    b) They have been practicing the dance routine all day.

    c) They have been watching the movie for an hour.

    d) They have been waiting for the bus for half an hour.

    e) They have been talking on the phone for hours.

Answers

    a) They worked on the project for weeks.

    b) They practiced the dance routine all day.

    c) They watched the movie for an hour.

    d) They waited for the bus for half an hour.

e) They talked on the phone for hours.

Exercise 20: Rewrite the sentences using a different tense

Questions

a) They have been walking in the park for an hour. for an hour.
b) They have been waiting for the movie to start.
c) They have been studying for the exam all day.
d) They have been playing chess for an hour.

Answers

a) They walked in the park
b) They waited for the movie to start.
c) They studied for the exam all day.
d) They played chess for an hour.

Chapter 17: Rewrite the sentence(s) using a different type of sentence

Exercise 1: Rewrite the sentence using a different type of sentence

Question

    a) The sun sets in the west.

Answer

    a) When the sun sets in the west, the sky turns a beautiful shade of orange and pink.

Chapter 18: Rewrite the following sentence(s) using an adverbial clause of time

Exercise 1: Rewrite the following sentence using an adverbial clause of time

Questions

    a) She finished her homework before she watched TV.
    b) She arrived early, so she had time to relax before the meeting.
    c) She studied for her test until midnight.
    d) She goes to the gym every morning.
    e) She finished the project before the deadline.
    f) She went to bed after she finished her book.

Answers

    a) After finishing her homework, she watched TV.
    b) She arrived early, giving her time to relax before the meeting.
    c) She studied for her test until midnight.
    d) She goes to the gym every morning.

e) She finished the project before the deadline.

f) She went to bed after she finished her book.

Chapter 19: Rewrite the following sentence(s) using a noun clause

Exercise 1: Rewrite the following sentence using a noun clause

Questions

a) The teacher said that the exam would be difficult.

Answer

a) The teacher's statement that the exam would be difficult worried the students.

Chapter 20: Rewrite the following sentence(s) using a participle phrase

Exercise 1: Rewrite the following sentence using a participle phrase

Question

a) The car, which was old and rusty, broke down on the highway.

Answer

a) The old and rusty car broke down on the highway.

Chapter 21: Rewrite the following sentence(s) using an infinitive phrase

Exercise 1: Rewrite the following sentences using an infinitive phrase

Questions

a) She wants to study abroad.
b) He tried to lift the heavy box.
c) She decided to take a nap.
d) He wants to eat pizza for dinner.
e) She decided to write a novel.

Answers

a) Her goal is to study abroad.
b) He attempted to lift the heavy box.
c) Her decision was to take a nap.
d) His desire is to eat pizza for dinner.
e) Her decision was to write a novel.

Exercise 2: Rewrite the following sentences using an infinitive phrase

Questions

a) He decided to take a break from work.
b) He wants to learn how to play the guitar.
c) She decided to start her own business.
d) He wants to buy a new car.
e) She decided to take a trip to Europe.

Answers

a) His decision was to take a break from work.
b) His desire is to learn how to play the guitar.

c) Her decision was to start her own business.

d) His desire is to buy a new car.

e) Her decision was to take a trip to Europe.

Exercise 3: Rewrite the following sentences using an infinitive phrase

Questions

a) He decided to quit his job.

b) She wants to become a doctor.

c) He wants to learn how to speak Spanish.

d) She wants to travel the world.

e) She wants to buy a new car.

Answers

a) His decision was to quit his job.

b) Her desire is to become a doctor.

c) His desire is to learn how to speak Spanish.

d) Her desire is to travel the world.

e) Her desire is to buy a new car.

Exercise 4: Rewrite the following sentences using an infinitive phrase

Questions

a) She decided to pursue a career in medicine.

b) She wants to write a book.

c) She wants to learn how to play the piano.

d) He wants to learn how to surf.

e) She wants to write a novel.

Answers

a) Her decision was to pursue a career in medicine.

b) Her desire is to write a book.

c) Her desire is to learn how to play the piano.

d) His desire is to learn how to surf.

e) Her desire is to write a novel.

Exercise 5: Rewrite the following sentences using an infinitive phrase

Questions

a) She wants to become a doctor.

b) She wants to learn how to play the guitar.

c) She wants to travel the world.

d) She wants to start her own business.

e) She wants to become a teacher.

Answers

a) Her desire is to become a doctor.

b) Her desire is to learn how to play the guitar.

c) Her desire is to travel the world.

d) Her desire is to start her own business.

e) Her desire is to become a teacher.

Exercise 6: Rewrite the following sentences using an infinitive phrase

Questions

a) She wants to learn how to swim.

b) She wants to learn how to cook.

c) She wants to learn how to play tennis.

d) She wants to learn how to speak French.

e) She wants to learn how to code.

Answers

a) Her desire is to learn how to swim.

b) Her desire is to learn how to cook.

c) Her desire is to learn how to play tennis.

d) Her desire is to learn how to speak French.

e) Her desire is to learn how to code.

Exercise 7: Rewrite the following sentences using an infinitive phrase

Questions

a) She wants to learn how to play the piano.

b) She wants to learn how to play chess.

c) She wants to learn how to ride a bike.

d) She wants to learn how to cook.

e) She wants to learn how to swim.

Answers

a) Her desire is to learn how to play the piano.

b) Her desire is to learn how to play chess.

c) Her desire is to learn how to ride a bike.

d) Her desire is to learn how to cook.

e) Her desire is to learn how to swim.

Exercise 8: Rewrite the following sentences using an infinitive phrase

Questions

a) She wants to learn how to paint.

b) She wants to learn how to play the guitar.

c) She wants to learn how to code.

d) She wants to learn how to dance.

e) She wants to learn how to sew.

Answers

a) Her desire is to learn how to paint.
b) Her desire is to learn how to play the guitar.
c) Her desire is to learn how to code.
d) Her desire is to learn how to dance.
e) Her desire is to learn how to sew.

Exercise 9: Rewrite the following sentences using an infinitive phrase

Questions

a) She wants to learn how to knit.
b) She wants to learn how to skateboard.
c) She wants to learn how to play the piano.
d) She wants to learn how to paint.
e) She wants to learn how to speak Spanish.

Answers

a) Her desire is to learn how to knit.
b) Her desire is to learn how to skateboard.
c) Her desire is to learn how to play the piano.
d) Her desire is to learn how to paint.
e) Her desire is to learn how to speak Spanish.

Exercise 10: Rewrite the following sentences using an infinitive phrase

Questions

a) She wants to learn how to surf.
b) She wants to learn how to dance.

c) She wants to learn how to play the guitar.

d) She wants to learn how to code.

e) She wants to learn how to dance.

Answers

a) Her desire is to learn how to surf.

b) Her desire is to learn how to dance.

c) Her desire is to learn how to play the guitar.

d) Her desire is to learn how to code.

e) Her desire is to learn how to dance.

Chapter 22: Rewrite the following sentence(s) using a comparative form

Exercise 1: Rewrite the following sentences using a comparative form

Questions

a) Her essay was good, but his was better.
b) His presentation was good, but hers was better.
c) Her essay was good, but his was better.
d) His presentation was good, but hers was better.
e) Her essay was good, but his was better.

Answers

a) His essay was better than hers.
b) Her presentation was better than his.
c) His essay was better than hers.
d) Her presentation was better than his.
e) His essay was better than hers.

Exercise 2: Rewrite the following sentences using a comparative form

Questions

a) My car is fast, but yours is faster.
b) My phone is good, but hers is better.
c) Her presentation was good, but his was better.
d) The movie was good, but the book was better.

Answers

a) My car is not as fast as yours.
b) Her phone is better than mine.

c) His presentation was better than hers.

d) The book was better than the movie.

Chapter 23: Rewrite the following sentence(s) using a passive voice

Exercise 1: Rewrite the following sentences using a passive voice

Questions

a) The chef cooked the meal in the kitchen.
b) The company designed the website.
c) The company built the skyscraper.
d) The company printed the brochure.
e) The company shipped the package to the customer.

Answers

a) The meal was cooked by the chef in the kitchen.
b) The website was designed by the company.
c) The skyscraper was built by the company.
d) The brochure was printed by the company.
e) The package was shipped to the customer by the company.

Exercise 2: Rewrite the following sentences using a passive voice

Questions

a) The company designed the logo.
b) The company manufactured the product.
c) The company assembled the product.
d) The company produced the movie.
e) The company developed the software.

Answers

a) The logo was designed by the company.
b) The product was manufactured by the company.

c) The product was assembled by the company.

d) The movie was produced by the company.

e) The software was developed by the company.

Exercise 3: Rewrite the following sentences using a passive voice

Questions

a) The company designed the website.

b) The company created the advertisement.

c) The company delivered the package.

d) The company sold the car.

e) The company built the factory.

Answers

a) The website was designed by the company.

b) The advertisement was created by the company.

c) The package was delivered by the company.

d) The car was sold by the company.

e) The factory was built by the company.

Exercise 4: Rewrite the following sentences using a passive voice

Questions

a) The company launched the product.

b) The company shipped the order.

c) The company produced the film.

d) The company hired the new employee.

e) The company designed the website.

Answers

a) The product was launched by the company.

b) The order was shipped by the company.

c) The film was produced by the company.

d) The new employee was hired by the company.

e) The website was designed by the company.

Exercise 5: Rewrite the following sentences using a passive voice

Questions

a) The company repaired the machine.

b) The dog ate the cake.

c) The chef prepared the meal.

d) The company hired the new employee.

e) The teacher gave the students a quiz.

Answers

a) The machine was repaired by the company.

b) The cake was eaten by the dog.

c) The meal was prepared by the chef.

d) The new employee was hired by the company.

e) The students were given a quiz by the teacher.

Exercise 6: Rewrite the following sentences using a passive voice

Questions

a) The company awarded her the prize.

b) The waiter served us our food.

c) The company sent her a letter.

d) The company awarded the contract to our firm.

e) The company paid the workers their salaries.

Answers

a) She was awarded the prize by the company.

b) We were served our food by the waiter.

c) She was sent a letter by the company.

d) Our firm was awarded the contract by the company.

e) The workers were paid their salaries by the company.

Exercise 7: Rewrite the following sentences using a passive voice

Questions

a) The police arrested the suspect.

b) The chef cooked the meal.

c) The teacher assigned the homework.

d) The waiter brought us our food.

e) The doctor performed the surgery.

Answers

a) The suspect was arrested by the police.

b) The meal was cooked by the chef.

c) The homework was assigned by the teacher.

d) We were brought our food by the waiter.

e) The surgery was performed by the doctor.

Exercise 8: Rewrite the following sentences using a passive voice

Questions

a) The company hired a new employee.

b) The company awarded him a bonus.

c) The company shipped the order yesterday.

d) The company delivered the package this morning.

e) The company sold the car for $10,000.

Answers

a) A new employee was hired by the company.

b) He was awarded a bonus by the company.

c) The order was shipped by the company yesterday.

d) The package was delivered by the company this morning.

e) The car was sold by the company for $10,000.

Exercise 9: Rewrite the following sentences using a passive voice

Questions

a) The company rejected his job application.

b) The chef cooked the meal.

c) The company designed the new product.

d) The company produced the goods in China.

e) The company developed the software.

Answers

a) His job application was rejected by the company.

b) The meal was cooked by the chef.

c) The new product was designed by the company.

d) The goods were produced by the company in China.

e) The software was developed by the company.

Exercise 10: Rewrite the following sentences using a passive voice

Questions

a) The company delivered the package on time.

b) The chef cooked the meal to perfection.

c) The company manufactured the product in China.

d) The company shipped the product to the customer.

e) The company produced the goods in India.

Answers

a) The package was delivered by the company on time.

b) The meal was cooked to perfection by the chef.

c) The product was manufactured by the company in China.

d) The product was shipped to the customer by the company.

e) The goods were produced by the company in India.

Chapter 24: Rewrite the following sentence(s) using a causative form

Exercise 1: Rewrite the following sentences using a causative form

Questions

a) The boss had the assistant make copies of the document.
b) The manager had the assistant create the presentation.
c) The boss had the assistant proofread the document.
d) The boss had the assistant book the flight.
e) The boss had the assistant buy the office supplies.

Answers

a) The boss made the assistant make copies of the document.
b) The manager made the assistant create the presentation.
c) The boss made the assistant proofread the document.
d) The boss made the assistant book the flight.
e) The boss made the assistant buy the office supplies.

Exercise 2: Rewrite the following sentences using a causative form

Questions

a) The boss had the assistant prepare the budget.
b) The boss had the assistant schedule the meeting.
c) The boss had the assistant draft the proposal.
d) The boss had the assistant proofread the report.
e) The boss had the assistant clean the office.

Answers

a) The boss made the assistant prepare the budget.
b) The boss made the assistant schedule the meeting.

c) The boss made the assistant draft the proposal.

d) The boss made the assistant proofread the report.

e) The boss made the assistant clean the office.

Exercise 3: Rewrite the following sentences using a causative form

Questions

a) The boss had the assistant file the paperwork.

b) The boss had the assistant organize the files.

c) The boss had the assistant book the flight.

d) The boss had the assistant write the email.

e) The boss had the assistant schedule the meeting.

Answers

a) The boss made the assistant file the paperwork.

b) The boss made the assistant organize the files.

c) The boss made the assistant book the flight.

d) The boss made the assistant write the email.

e) The boss made the assistant schedule the meeting.

Exercise 4: Rewrite the following sentences using a causative form

Questions

a) The boss had the assistant prepare the presentation.

b) The boss had the assistant print the documents.

c) The boss had the assistant make the coffee.

d) The boss had the assistant buy the office supplies.

e) The boss had the assistant send the email.

Answers

a) The boss made the assistant prepare the presentation.

b) The boss made the assistant print the documents.

c) The boss made the assistant make the coffee.

d) The boss made the assistant buy the office supplies.

e) The boss made the assistant send the email.

Exercise 5: Rewrite the following sentences using a causative form

Questions

a) The boss had the assistant make copies of the report.

b) The boss had the assistant type the letter.

c) The teacher made the students study for the exam.

d) The boss had his assistant schedule the meeting.

e) The doctor had the patient take the medicine.

Answers

a) The boss made the assistant make copies of the report.

b) The boss made the assistant type the letter.

c) The teacher had the students study for the exam.

d) The boss got his assistant to schedule the meeting.

e) The doctor made the patient take the medicine.

Exercise 5: Rewrite the following sentences using a causative form

Questions

a) The mechanic fixed the car.

b) The teacher had the students write an essay.

c) The doctor had the patient undergo surgery.

d) The coach had the team practice for hours.

e) The manager had the staff work overtime.

Answers

a) The mechanic had the car fixed.

b) The teacher made the students write an essay.

c) The doctor made the patient undergo surgery.

d) The coach made the team practice for hours.

e) The manager made the staff work overtime.

Exercise 6: Rewrite the following sentences using a causative form

Questions

a) The boss had the secretary make copies.

b) The landlord had the plumber fix the leaky faucet.

c) The company had the team work overtime.

d) The coach had the team run laps.

e) The boss had the assistant organize the files.

Answers

a) The boss made the secretary make copies.

b) The landlord made the plumber fix the leaky faucet.

c) The company made the team work overtime.

d) The coach made the team run laps.

e) The boss made the assistant organize the files.

Exercise 7: Rewrite the following sentences using a causative form

Questions

a) The teacher had the students complete the assignment.

b) The doctor had the nurse take the patient's temperature.

c) The teacher had the students read the book.

d) The boss had the assistant make copies of the report.

e) The company had the employees complete a survey.

Answers

a) The teacher made the students complete the assignment.
b) The doctor made the nurse take the patient's temperature.
c) The teacher made the students read the book.
d) The boss made the assistant make copies of the report.
e) The company made the employees complete a survey.

Exercise 8: Rewrite the following sentences using a causative form

Questions

a) The teacher had the students write an essay.
b) The boss had the employees attend a training session.
c) The manager had the employees clean the office.
d) The teacher had the students take a test.
e) The boss had the assistant book the flight.

Answers

a) The teacher made the students write an essay.
b) The boss made the employees attend a training session.
c) The manager made the employees clean the office.
d) The teacher made the students take a test.
e) The boss made the assistant book the flight.

Exercise 9: Rewrite the following sentences using a causative form

Questions

a) The manager had the employees prepare the report.
b) The boss had the assistant prepare the agenda.

c) The teacher had the students read a chapter.

d) The manager had the assistant schedule the meeting.

e) The boss had the assistant write the report.

Answers

a) The manager made the employees prepare the report.

b) The boss made the assistant prepare the agenda.

c) The teacher made the students read a chapter.

d) The manager made the assistant schedule the meeting.

e) The boss made the assistant write the report.

Chapter 25: Rewrite the following sentence(s) using a conditional sentence

Exercise 1: Rewrite the following sentences using a conditional sentence

Questions

a) If it snows, we will go skiing.
b) If I win the lottery, I will travel the world.
c) If I finish my work early, I will go to the gym.
d) If I wake up early, I will go for a run.
e) If I finish my homework, I will watch a movie.

Answers

a) We will go skiing if it snows.
b) I will travel the world if I win the lottery.
c) I will go to the gym if I finish my work early.
d) I will go for a run if I wake up early.
e) I will watch a movie if I finish my homework.

Exercise 2: Rewrite the following sentences using a conditional sentence

Questions

a) If I get the promotion, I will buy a new car.
b) If I win the lottery, I will buy a house.
c) If I have time, I will read a book.
d) If I have enough money, I will buy a new phone.
e) If I get the job, I will move to a new city.

Answers

a) I will buy a new car if I get the promotion.

b) I will buy a house if I win the lottery.

c) I will read a book if I have time.

d) I will buy a new phone if I have enough money.

e) I will move to a new city if I get the job.

Exercise 3: Rewrite the following sentences using a conditional sentence

Questions

a) If it's sunny, we will go to the beach.

b) If I have enough time, I will take a nap.

c) If it snows, we will build a snowman.

d) If I see him, I will say hello.

e) If I win the lottery, I will travel the world.

Answers

a) We will go to the beach if it's sunny.

b) I will take a nap if I have enough time.

c) We will build a snowman if it snows.

d) I will say hello if I see him.

e) I will travel the world if I win the lottery.

Exercise 4: Rewrite the following sentences using a conditional sentence

Questions

a) If it rains, we will stay indoors.

b) If I get a promotion, I will buy a new car.

c) If I have time, I will call you.

d) If I save enough money, I will buy a house.

e) If I study hard, I will get good grades.

Answers

a) We will stay indoors if it rains.

b) I will buy a new car if I get a promotion.

c) I will call you if I have time.

d) I will buy a house if I save enough money.

e) I will get good grades if I study hard.

Exercise 5: Rewrite the following sentences using a conditional sentence

Questions

a) If I win the competition, I will receive a prize.

b) If it rains, we will stay home.

c) She won't go to the party if she doesn't finish her work.

d) If I have time, I will go to the gym.

e) She will buy the dress if it's on sale.

Answers

a) I will receive a prize if I win the competition.

b) We will stay home if it rains.

c) If she doesn't finish her work, she won't go to the party.

d) I will go to the gym if I have time.

e) If the dress is on sale, she will buy it.

Exercise 6: Rewrite the following sentences using a conditional sentence

Questions

a) If I see him, I will let him know.

b) I will buy the dress if it fits me.

c) If I win the lottery, I will buy a house.

d) If I have time, I will call you.

e) If it snows, we will go skiing.

Answers

a) I will let him know if I see him.

b) If the dress fits me, I will buy it.

c) I will buy a house if I win the lottery.

d) I will call you if I have time.

e) We will go skiing if it snows.

Exercise 7: Rewrite the following sentences using a conditional sentence

Questions

a) If the restaurant is busy, we might have to wait for a table.

b) If I had more money, I would travel more often.

c) If you need any help, just ask.

d) If it rains, we will stay inside.

e) If I go to the party, I will wear my new dress.

Answers

a) We might have to wait for a table if the restaurant is busy.

b) I would travel more often if I had more money.

c) Just ask if you need any help.

d) We will stay inside if it rains.

e) I will wear my new dress if I go to the party.

Exercise 8: Rewrite the following sentences using a conditional sentence

Questions

a) If it's hot outside, we will go to the beach.

b) If I have time, I will go to the gym.

c) If I win the lottery, I will travel the world.

d) If I finish my work early, I will go for a walk.

e) If I don't finish my work on time, I will have to stay late.

Answers

a) We will go to the beach if it's hot outside.
b) I will go to the gym if I have time.
c) I will travel the world if I win the lottery.
d) I will go for a walk if I finish my work early.
e) I will have to stay late if I don't finish my work on time.

Exercise 9: Rewrite the following sentences using a conditional sentence

Questions

a) If I wake up early, I will go for a run.
b) If I see him, I will tell him the news.
c) If I have time, I will call you.
d) If it rains tomorrow, I will stay inside.
e) If I have enough money, I will buy a new car.

Answers

a) I will go for a run if I wake up early.
b) I will tell him the news if I see him.
c) I will call you if I have time.
d) I will stay inside if it rains tomorrow.
e) I will buy a new car if I have enough money.

Exercise 10: Rewrite the following sentences using a conditional sentence

Questions

a) If I have time, I will read a book.
b) If it snows, we will build a snowman.

c) If I have enough money, I will go on vacation.

d) If I get the job, I will move to a new city.

Answers

a) I will read a book if I have time.

b) We will build a snowman if it snows.

c) I will go on vacation if I have enough money.

d) I will move to a new city if I get the job.

Chapter 26: Rewrite the following sentence(s) using an appositive phrase

Exercise 1: Rewrite the following sentences using an appositive phrase

Questions

a) My best friend, who is a doctor, is coming to visit.
b) The book, which is about ancient civilizations, is very interesting.
c) My friend, who is a musician, is performing tonight.
d) My neighbor, who is a retired teacher, is very friendly.
e) My favorite actor, who starred in that movie, won an award.

Answers

a) My best friend, a doctor, is coming to visit.
b) The book, about ancient civilizations, is very interesting.
c) My musician friend is performing tonight.
d) My retired teacher neighbor is very friendly.
e) The actor I like best, who starred in that movie, won an award.

Exercise 2: Rewrite the following sentences using an appositive phrase

Questions

a) My teacher, who is also a writer, gave me some great advice.
b) My friend, who is a lawyer, gave me some legal advice.
c) My neighbor, who is a retired police officer, is very helpful.
d) My favorite author, who wrote that book, will be speaking at the event.
e) My professor, who is an expert in her field, wrote a book on the subject.

Answers

a) My teacher, a writer, gave me some great advice.

b) My lawyer friend gave me some legal advice.

c) My retired police officer neighbor is very helpful.

d) The author I like best, who wrote that book, will be speaking at the event.

e) My professor, an expert in her field, wrote a book on the subject.

Exercise 3: Rewrite the following sentences using an appositive phrase

Questions

a) My doctor, who is also a friend, gave me some medical advice.

b) My boss, who is the CEO, gave a speech at the conference.

c) My favorite singer, who released a new album, will be performing at the concert.

d) My neighbor, who is a doctor, helped me when I was sick.

e) My best friend, who is a lawyer, helped me with my legal problem.

Answers

a) My friend, the doctor, gave me some medical advice.

b) My boss, the CEO, gave a speech at the conference.

c) The singer I like best, who released a new album, will be performing at the concert.

d) My doctor neighbor helped me when I was sick.

e) My lawyer best friend helped me with my legal problem.

Exercise 4: Rewrite the following sentences using an appositive phrase

Questions

a) My sister, who is a musician, will be performing at the concert.

b) My favorite actor, who won an Academy Award, will be in the new movie.

c) My favorite author, who wrote my favorite book, will be at the book signing.

d) My favorite musician, who won a Grammy award, will perform at the concert.

e) My favorite actor, who starred in my favorite movie, will be at the film festival.

Answers

a) My musician sister will be performing at the concert.
b) The actor I like best, who won an Academy Award, will be in the new movie.
c) The author I like best, who wrote my favorite book, will be at the book signing.
d) The musician I like best, who won a Grammy award, will perform at the concert.
e) The actor I like best, who starred in my favorite movie, will be at the film festival.

Exercise 5: Rewrite the following sentences using an appositive phrase

Questions

a) My favorite artist, who painted my favorite painting, will be at the art exhibit.
b) My favorite author, who wrote my favorite book, will be speaking at the book festival.
c) My favorite musician, who wrote my favorite song, will perform at the concert.
d) My favorite athlete, who won a gold medal, will compete in the Olympics.
e) My favorite author, who wrote my favorite book, will give a speech at the literary festival.

Answers

a) The artist I like best, who painted my favorite painting, will be at the art exhibit.
b) The author I like best, who wrote my favorite book, will be speaking at the book festival.
c) The musician I like best, who wrote my favorite song, will perform at the concert.
d) The athlete I like best, who won a gold medal, will compete in the Olympics.
e) The author I like best, who wrote my favorite book, will give a speech at the literary festival.

Exercise 6: Rewrite the following sentences using an appositive phrase

Questions

a) My favorite actor, who starred in my favorite movie, will be in the new film.
b) My favorite artist, who painted my favorite painting, will be featured in the art exhibit.
c) My favorite musician, who wrote my favorite song, will perform at the music festival.
d) My favorite actor, who starred in my favorite movie, will attend the film festival.
e) My favorite musician, who wrote my favorite song, will release a new album.

Answers

a) The actor I like best, who starred in my favorite movie, will be in the new film.
b) The artist I like best, who painted my favorite painting, will be featured in the art exhibit.
c) The musician I like best, who wrote my favorite song, will perform at the music festival.
d) The actor I like best, who starred in my favorite movie, will attend the film festival.
e) The musician I like best, who wrote my favorite song, will release a new album.

Exercise 7: Rewrite the following sentences using an appositive phrase

Questions

a) My favorite actor, who starred in my favorite movie, will receive an award.
b) My favorite artist, who painted my favorite artwork, will have a solo exhibition.
c) My favorite musician, who wrote my favorite song, will perform at the concert.
d) My favorite actor, who starred in my favorite movie, will direct a new film.
e) My favorite author, who wrote my favorite book, will publish a new novel.

Answers

a) The actor I like best, who starred in my favorite movie, will receive an award.
b) The artist I like best, who painted my favorite artwork, will have a solo exhibition.
c) The musician I like best, who wrote my favorite song, will perform at the concert.
d) The actor I like best, who starred in my favorite movie, will direct a new film.
e) The author I like best, who wrote my favorite book, will publish a new novel.

Exercise 8: Rewrite the following sentences using an appositive phrase

Questions

a) My favorite painter, who created my favorite artwork, will have an exhibition.
b) My favorite singer, who performed my favorite song, will release a new album.
c) My favorite poet, who wrote my favorite poem, will publish a new book.
d) My favorite actor, who starred in my favorite movie, will receive an award.
e) My favorite athlete, who won my favorite game, will retire soon.

Answers

a) The painter I like best, who created my favorite artwork, will have an exhibition.
b) The singer I like best, who performed my favorite song, will release a new album.
c) The poet I like best, who wrote my favorite poem, will publish a new book.
d) The actor I like best, who starred in my favorite movie, will receive an award.
e) The athlete I like best, who won my favorite game, will retire soon.

Exercise 9: Rewrite the following sentences using an appositive phrase

Questions

a) My favorite musician, who wrote my favorite song, will release a new album.

b) My favorite director, who made my favorite movie, will direct a new film.

c) My favorite author, who wrote my favorite book, will publish a new novel.

d) My favorite artist, who painted my favorite picture, will have an exhibition.

e) My favorite actor, who starred in my favorite TV show, will appear in a new series.

Answers

a) The musician I like best, who wrote my favorite song, will release a new album.

b) The director I like best, who made my favorite movie, will direct a new film.

c) The author I like best, who wrote my favorite book, will publish a new novel.

d) The artist I like best, who painted my favorite picture, will have an exhibition.

e) The actor I like best, who starred in my favorite TV show, will appear in a new series.

Exercise 10: Rewrite the following sentences using an appositive phrase

Questions

a) My favorite singer, who wrote my favorite song, will perform at the concert.

b) My favorite poet, who wrote my favorite poem, will give a reading.

c) My favorite athlete, who won my favorite game, will compete in a tournament.

d) My favorite musician, who composed my favorite song, will release a new album.

e) My favorite director, who made my favorite movie, will release a new film.

Answers

a) The singer I like best, who wrote my favorite song, will perform at the concert.

b) The poet I like best, who wrote my favorite poem, will give a reading.

c) The athlete I like best, who won my favorite game, will compete in a tournament.

d) The musician I like best, who composed my favorite song, will release a new album.

e) The director I like best, who made my favorite movie, will release a new film.

Chapter 27: Rewrite the following sentence(s)using a gerund phrase

Exercise 1: Rewrite the following sentences using a gerund phrase

Questions

a) She is interested in learning Spanish.
b) He enjoys playing video games with his friends.
c) She spends her weekends hiking in the mountains.
d) She loves listening to music on her phone.
e) He spends his evenings watching TV.

Answers

a) Her interest lies in learning Spanish.
b) Playing video games with his friends is his favorite pastime.
c) Hiking in the mountains is how she spends her weekends.
d) Listening to music on her phone is her favorite hobby.
e) Watching TV is how he spends his evenings.

Exercise 2: Rewrite the following sentences using a gerund phrase

Questions

a) He likes to swim in the ocean.
b) She enjoys running in the park.
c) He spends his weekends playing basketball.
d) She enjoys taking long walks in the countryside.
e) She enjoys reading books in her free time.

Answers

a) Swimming in the ocean is something he likes.
b) Running in the park is something she enjoys.

c) Playing basketball is how he spends his weekends.

d) Taking long walks in the countryside is something she enjoys.

e) Reading books in her free time is something she enjoys.

Exercise 3: Rewrite the following sentences using a gerund phrase

Questions

a) She enjoys cooking meals for her family.

b) He enjoys playing video games in his free time.

c) She enjoys taking photographs of nature.

d) He enjoys playing the guitar in his free time.

e) She enjoys painting landscapes.

Answers

a) Cooking meals for her family is something she enjoys.

b) Playing video games in his free time is something he enjoys.

c) Taking photographs of nature is something she enjoys.

d) Playing the guitar in his free time is something he enjoys.

e) Painting landscapes is something she enjoys.

Exercise 4: Rewrite the following sentences using a gerund phrase

Questions

a) He enjoys playing basketball on the weekends.

b) She enjoys dancing salsa.

c) He enjoys reading science fiction novels.

d) She enjoys hiking in the mountains.

e) He enjoys playing video games.

Answers

a) Playing basketball on the weekends is something he enjoys.

b) Dancing salsa is something she enjoys.

c) Reading science fiction novels is something he enjoys.

d) Hiking in the mountains is something she enjoys.

e) Playing video games is something he enjoys.

Exercise 5: Rewrite the following sentences using a gerund phrase

Questions

a) She enjoys watching movies on the weekends.

b) She enjoys writing poetry.

c) He enjoys playing the guitar.

d) She enjoys painting landscapes.

e) He enjoys playing basketball.

Answers

a) Watching movies on the weekends is something she enjoys.

b) Writing poetry is something she enjoys.

c) Playing the guitar is something he enjoys.

d) Painting landscapes is something she enjoys.

e) Playing basketball is something he enjoys.

Exercise 6: Rewrite the following sentences using a gerund phrase

Questions

a) She enjoys reading novels.

b) He enjoys swimming in the ocean.

c) She enjoys hiking in the mountains.

d) He enjoys playing soccer.

e) She enjoys playing tennis.

Answers

a) Reading novels is something she enjoys.
b) Swimming in the ocean is something he enjoys.
c) Hiking in the mountains is something she enjoys.
d) Playing soccer is something he enjoys.
e) Playing tennis is something she enjoys.

Exercise 7: Rewrite the following sentences using a gerund phrase

Questions

a) He enjoys playing guitar.
b) She enjoys singing in the choir.
c) He enjoys playing basketball.
d) She enjoys reading books.
e) He enjoys playing video games.

Answers

a) Playing guitar is something he enjoys.
b) Singing in the choir is something she enjoys.
c) Playing basketball is something he enjoys.
d) Reading books is something she enjoys.
e) Playing video games is something he enjoys.

Exercise 8: Rewrite the following sentences using a gerund phrase

Questions

a) She enjoys watching movies.
b) He enjoys hiking in the mountains.
c) She enjoys writing poetry.
d) He enjoys playing soccer.

e) She enjoys cooking.

Answers

a) Watching movies is something she enjoys.

b) Hiking in the mountains is something he enjoys.

c) Writing poetry is something she enjoys.

d) Playing soccer is something he enjoys.

e) Cooking is something she enjoys.

Exercise 9: Rewrite the following sentences using a gerund phrase

Questions

a) He enjoys playing basketball.

b) She enjoys singing.

c) He enjoys reading books.

d) She enjoys playing the guitar.

e) He enjoys playing video games.

Answers

a) Playing basketball is something he enjoys.

b) Singing is something she enjoys.

c) Reading books is something he enjoys.

d) Playing the guitar is something she enjoys.

e) Playing video games is something he enjoys.

Exercise 10: Rewrite the following sentences using a gerund phrase

Questions

a) She enjoys hiking.

b) He enjoys playing soccer.

c) She enjoys reading books in her spare time.

Answers

a) Hiking is something she enjoys.
b) Playing soccer is something he enjoys.
c) Her favorite pastime is reading books.

Chapter 28: Rewrite the following sentence(s) using a relative clause

Chapter 1: Rewrite the following sentences using a relative clause

Questions

a) The woman is talking to the man. He is wearing a blue shirt.
b) The girl is reading a book. The book is about space.
c) The house that is on the corner is for sale.
d) The dress that she bought is very pretty.
e) The woman who is wearing the blue dress is my sister.

Answers

a) The woman who is talking is speaking to the man wearing a blue shirt.
b) The girl who is reading a book is reading a book about space.
c) The house for sale is the one that is on the corner.
d) The dress she bought is very pretty.
e) My sister is the woman who is wearing the blue dress.

Chapter 2: Rewrite the following sentences using a relative clause

Questions

a) The car that is parked in front of the house is mine.
b) The man who is standing over there is my boss.
c) The movie that we saw last night was very good.
d) The woman who is wearing a red dress is my cousin.
e) The book that she recommended is very interesting.

Answers

a) The car parked in front of the house is mine.
b) My boss is the man who is standing over there.

c) The movie we saw last night was very good.

d) My cousin is the woman who is wearing a red dress.

e) The book she recommended is very interesting.

Chapter 3: Rewrite the following sentences using a relative clause

Questions

a) The dog that is barking loudly is mine.

b) The car that is parked in the driveway is mine.

c) The book that I read last night was very interesting.

d) The woman who is wearing a yellow dress is my neighbor.

e) The man who is wearing a blue shirt is my brother.

Answers

a) The dog that is barking loudly is mine.

b) The car parked in the driveway is mine.

c) The book I read last night was very interesting.

d) My neighbor is the woman who is wearing a yellow dress.

e) My brother is the man who is wearing a blue shirt.

Chapter 4: Rewrite the following sentences using a relative clause

Questions

a) The woman who is wearing a green hat is my friend.

b) The man who is wearing a hat is the tour guide.

c) The woman who is wearing a red dress is the teacher.

d) The man who is wearing a suit is the CEO.

e) The woman who is wearing a black dress is the singer.

Answers

a) My friend is the woman who is wearing a green hat.

b) The tour guide is the man who is wearing a hat.

c) The teacher is the woman who is wearing a red dress.

d) The CEO is the man who is wearing a suit.

e) The singer is the woman who is wearing a black dress.

Chapter 5: Rewrite the following sentences using a relative clause

Questions

a) The man who is wearing a tie is the lawyer.

b) The woman who is wearing a necklace is my sister.

c) The man who is wearing a hat is the professor.

d) The woman who is wearing a blue dress is the manager.

e) The man who is wearing a red shirt is the doctor.

Answers

a) The lawyer is the man who is wearing a tie.

b) My sister is the woman who is wearing a necklace.

c) The professor is the man who is wearing a hat.

d) The manager is the woman who is wearing a blue dress.

e) The doctor is the man who is wearing a red shirt.

Chapter 6: Rewrite the following sentences using a relative clause

Questions

a) The woman who is wearing a green dress is the teacher.

b) The man who is wearing a blue shirt is the banker.

c) The woman who is wearing a yellow shirt is the CEO.

d) The man who is wearing a black suit is the lawyer.

e) The woman who is wearing a purple dress is the nurse.

Answers

a) The teacher is the woman who is wearing a green dress.

b) The banker is the man who is wearing a blue shirt.

c) The CEO is the woman who is wearing a yellow shirt.

d) The lawyer is the man who is wearing a black suit.

e) The nurse is the woman who is wearing a purple dress.

Chapter 7: Rewrite the following sentences using a relative clause

Questions

a) The man who is wearing a gray suit is the accountant.

b) The woman who is wearing a pink dress is the receptionist.

c) The man who is wearing a brown suit is the manager.

d) The woman who is wearing a green dress is the teacher.

e) The man who is wearing a blue shirt is the doctor.

Answers

a) The accountant is the man who is wearing a gray suit.

b) The receptionist is the woman who is wearing a pink dress.

c) The manager is the man who is wearing a brown suit.

d) The teacher is the woman who is wearing a green dress.

e) The doctor is the man who is wearing a blue shirt.

Chapter 8: Rewrite the following sentences using a relative clause

Questions

a) The woman who is wearing a yellow dress is the salesperson.

b) The man who is wearing a red tie is the lawyer.

c) The woman who is wearing a purple dress is the artist.

d) The man who is wearing a black suit is the CEO.

e) The woman who is wearing a pink dress is the receptionist.

Answers

a) The salesperson is the woman who is wearing a yellow dress.
b) The lawyer is the man who is wearing a red tie.
c) The artist is the woman who is wearing a purple dress.
d) The CEO is the man who is wearing a black suit.
e) The receptionist is the woman who is wearing a pink dress.

Chapter 9: Rewrite the following sentences using a relative clause

Questions

a) The man who is wearing a brown jacket is the engineer.
b) The woman who is wearing a green dress is the teacher.
c) The man who is wearing a gray suit is the accountant.
d) The woman who is wearing a blue dress is the librarian.
e) The man who is wearing a red shirt is the salesman.

Answers

a) The engineer is the man who is wearing a brown jacket.
b) The teacher is the woman who is wearing a green dress.
c) The accountant is the man who is wearing a gray suit.
d) The librarian is the woman who is wearing a blue dress.
e) The salesman is the man who is wearing a red shirt.

Chapter 10: Rewrite the following sentences using a relative clause

Questions

a) The woman who is wearing a purple dress is the doctor.
b) The man who is wearing a black suit is the lawyer.

Answers

a) The doctor is the woman who is wearing a purple dress.

b) The lawyer is the man who is wearing a black suit.

Chapter 29: Rewrite the following sentence(s)using an imperative

Exercise 1: Rewrite the following sentences using an imperative

Questions

a) You should always wear a seatbelt.
b) Please be quiet during the movie.
c) Don't forget to turn off the lights before you leave.
d) Please don't smoke in the building.
e) Don't be late for your appointment.

Answers

a) Wear a seatbelt at all times.
b) Keep quiet during the movie, please.
c) Remember to turn off the lights before you leave.
d) Do not smoke in the building, please.
e) Be on time for your appointment, please.

Exercise 2: Rewrite the following sentences using an imperative

Questions

a) Please keep off the grass.
b) Please don't touch the art.
c) Please turn off the lights when you leave.
d) Don't forget to bring your passport to the airport.
e) Please be careful when you cross the street.

Answers

a) Do not walk on the grass, please.
b) Do not touch the art, please.

c) Turn off the lights when you leave, please.

d) Remember to bring your passport to the airport.

e) Be careful when you cross the street, please.

Exercise 3: Rewrite the following sentences using an imperative

Questions

a) Please keep the noise down.

b) Please don't forget to lock the door.

c) Please be quiet while the baby is sleeping.

d) Please don't talk during the movie.

e) Please turn off your cell phone during the meeting.

Answers

a) Keep the noise down, please.

b) Don't forget to lock the door, please.

c) Be quiet while the baby is sleeping, please.

d) Don't talk during the movie, please.

e) Turn off your cell phone during the meeting, please.

Exercise 4: Rewrite the following sentences using an imperative

Questions

a) Please don't smoke in the building.

b) Please don't eat in the library.

c) Please don't interrupt me while I'm speaking.

d) Please don't touch the artwork.

e) Please don't forget to buy milk.

Answers

a) Don't smoke in the building, please.

b) Don't eat in the library, please.

c) Don't interrupt me while I'm speaking, please.

d) Don't touch the artwork, please.

e) Don't forget to buy milk, please.

Exercise 5: Rewrite the following sentences using an imperative

Questions

a) Please don't park in the handicapped space.

b) Please don't leave the door open.

c) Please don't talk during the movie.

d) Please don't forget to turn off the lights.

e) Please don't smoke in the building.

Answers

a) Don't park in the handicapped space, please.

b) Don't leave the door open, please.

c) Don't talk during the movie, please.

d) Don't forget to turn off the lights, please.

e) Don't smoke in the building, please.

Exercise 6: Rewrite the following sentences using an imperative

Questions

a) Please don't be late for the meeting.

b) Please don't forget to lock the door.

c) Please don't eat in the library.

d) Please don't interrupt me while I'm speaking.

e) Please don't touch the artwork.

Answers

a) Don't be late for the meeting, please.

b) Don't forget to lock the door, please.

c) Don't eat in the library, please.

d) Don't interrupt me while I'm speaking, please.

e) Don't touch the artwork, please.

Exercise 7: Rewrite the following sentences using an imperative

Questions

a) Please don't forget to turn off the lights.

b) Please don't smoke in the building.

c) Please don't touch the hot stove.

d) Please don't talk during the movie.

e) Please don't eat in the library.

Answers

a) Don't forget to turn off the lights, please.

b) Don't smoke in the building, please.

c) Don't touch the hot stove, please.

d) Don't talk during the movie, please.

e) Don't eat in the library, please.

Exercise 8: Rewrite the following sentences using an imperative

Questions

a) Please don't leave the door open.

b) Please don't be late for the meeting.

c) Please don't forget to lock the door.

d) Please don't forget to turn off the lights.

e) Please don't interrupt me when I'm speaking.

Answers

a) Don't leave the door open, please.

b) Don't be late for the meeting, please.

c) Don't forget to lock the door, please.

d) Don't forget to turn off the lights, please.

e) Don't interrupt me when I'm speaking, please.

Exercise 9: Rewrite the following sentences using an imperative

Questions

a) Please don't smoke in the building.

b) Please don't talk during the movie.

c) Please don't touch the artwork.

d) Please don't run in the hallway.

e) Please don't forget to take out the trash.

Answers

a) Don't smoke in the building, please.

b) Don't talk during the movie, please.

c) Don't touch the artwork, please.

d) Don't run in the hallway, please.

e) Don't forget to take out the trash, please.

Exercise 10: Rewrite the following sentences using an imperative

Questions

a) Please don't touch the hot stove.

b) Please don't be late for the meeting.

c) Please don't forget to lock the door.

Answers

a) Don't touch the hot stove, please.
b) Don't be late for the meeting, please.
c) Don't forget to lock the door, please.

Chapter 30: Rewrite the following sentence(s) using an adverbial clause of reason

Exercise 1: Rewrite the following sentences using an adverbial clause of reason

Questions

a) She couldn't come to the party because she was sick.
b) She missed the bus because she overslept.
c) She missed the train because she overslept.
d) She stayed home because she was sick.
e) She left early because she was feeling sick.
f) She went to the doctor because she was feeling sick.

Answers

a) Since she was sick, she couldn't come to the party.
b) She missed the bus because she overslept.
c) She missed the train because she overslept.
d) She stayed home because she was sick.
e) She left early because she was feeling sick.
f) She went to the doctor because she was feeling sick.

Chapter 31: Rewrite the following sentence(s) using an adverbial clause of condition

Exercise 1: Rewrite the following sentences using an adverbial clause of condition

Questions

a) She will come to the party if she finishes her work.
b) He will go to the party if he finishes his work on time.
c) She will attend the party if she finishes her work on time.
d) She will go to the party if she finishes her work.
e) If it rains, we will stay inside.
f) She will go to the concert if she can get a ticket.

Answers

a) If she finishes her work, she will come to the party.
b) If he finishes his work on time, he will go to the party.
c) If she finishes her work on time, she will attend the party.
d) She will go to the party if she finishes her work.
e) We will stay inside if it rains.
f) If she can get a ticket, she will go to the concert.

Chapter 32: Rewrite the following sentence(s) using an adverbial clause of concession

Exercise 1: Rewrite the following sentences using an adverbial clause of concession

Questions

a) Although he was tired, he stayed up late.
b) Even though he was tired, he stayed up to finish his work.
c) Although he is very busy, he always finds time to exercise.
d) Although it was raining, she went for a walk.
e) Even though she was tired, she went to the gym.

Answers

a) Although he was tired, he stayed up late.
b) Although he was tired, he stayed up to finish his work.
c) He always finds time to exercise, although he is very busy.
d) Although it was raining, she went for a walk.
e) Even though she was tired, she went to the gym.

Chapter 33: Rewrite the following sentence(s) using an adverbial clause of manner

Exercise 1: Rewrite the following sentence using an adverbial clause of manner

Questions

a) She drove to the airport carefully.
b) She spoke to him in a gentle tone.
c) She sings beautifully.
d) She won the race by running very fast.
e) She drives her car carefully.
f) She sings beautifully.

Answers

a) She drove to the airport carefully.
b) She spoke to him in a gentle tone.
c) She sings beautifully, as if she were an angel.
d) She won the race by running very fast.
e) She drives her car carefully.
f) She sings beautifully.

Chapter 34: Rewrite the following sentence(s) using an adverbial clause of place

Exercise 1: Rewrite the following sentence using an adverbial clause of place

Questions

a) She looked for her keys where she usually keeps them.
b) She found her keys where she left them.
c) They had a picnic in the park.
d) She looked for her keys in the living room.
e) She went to the beach to swim.

Answers

a) She looked for her keys where she usually keeps them.
b) She found her keys where she left them.
c) They had a picnic in the park where they could enjoy the sunshine.
d) She looked for her keys in the living room.
e) She went to the beach to swim.

Chapter 35: Rewrite the following sentence(s) using an adverbial clause of purpose

Exercise 1: Rewrite the following sentence using an adverbial clause of purpose

Questions

   a) She studies hard so that she can get good grades.
   b) She went to the store to buy some milk.
   c) She went to the store to buy some groceries.
   d) She went to the library to study for her exam.
   e) She went to the store to buy some groceries.
   f) She went to the store to buy some milk.

Answers

   a) She studies hard so that she can get good grades.
   b) She went to the store to buy some milk.
   c) She went to the store so that she could buy some groceries.
   d) She went to the library to study for her exam.
   e) She went to the store to buy some groceries.
   f) She went to the store to buy some milk.

Chapter 36: Rewrite the following sentence(s) using an adverbial clause of result

Exercise 1: Rewrite the following sentence using an adverbial clause of result

Questions

a) She studied hard and earned an A.
b) He studied hard and got a good grade.
c) He worked hard, so he passed the exam.

Answers

a) She studied hard and earned an A.
b) He studied hard, with the result that he got a good grade.
c) He worked hard, so he passed the exam.

Chapter 37: Rewrite the following sentence(s) using an adverbial clause of contrast

Exercise 1: Rewrite the following sentences using an adverbial clause of contrast

Questions

a) He likes to work alone, although he enjoys being with people.
b) He is tall, but his brother is short.
c) Although he is rich, he is not happy.
d) Although it was cold outside, she wore a short-sleeved shirt.
e) She likes coffee, but he prefers tea.

Answers

a) Although he enjoys being with people, he likes to work alone.
b) He is tall, but his brother is short.
c) Although he is rich, he is not happy.
d) Although it was cold outside, she wore a short-sleeved shirt.
e) Although she likes coffee, he prefers tea.

Conclusion

Thank you once again for purchasing this book. I hope it has helped you in your journey to understanding sentence transformation.

Please, if you learnt something from this book, I would like you to leave a review. It'd be appreciated.

Thank you.

Printed in Great Britain
by Amazon